Overcoming Anxiety

A Single Idea Can Make a Difference

T S Gill MD

Shaleen K Gill MD

Sahiba Singh MD

Do not let the world make you hard. Do not let pain make you hate. Do not let the bitterness steal your sweetness. Take pride that even though the rest of the world may disagree, you still believe it to be a beautiful place

- Kurt Vonnegut

Disclaimer

No book can replace the services of a qualified health professional. Please use this book to help you communicate more effectively with your doctor so that you can obtain the best possible care. This book is not intended as a guide for self-medication. Pharmacological treatments are discussed to provide information that may be useful in discussing your treatment with the prescribing doctor. Over the counter medications and herbs can interact with other medications and should be discussed with your doctor. The author and publisher expressly disclaim responsibility for any negative effects directly or indirectly attributable to the use or application of any information contained in this book

Dedication

To my Mother

Surjit K Gill (1943-1985)

Acknowledgements

My mother lost both her parents at a young age and was later adopted by her uncle. She went through a lot in her short years. To me, she was a pillar of strength and resolve and never dwelt on struggles. There were times, though, when her past despair came out of the shadows and she shared the anxieties she had suffered as a child. I am dedicating this book to her.

I would like to also acknowledge my wife, Baljeet, for encouraging me to put my own thoughts on paper about the subject. She has been a source of support and strength over the years.

Dr. Shaleen Gill helped me do some of the background research in alternative therapies. I am grateful to her for her contributions.

Dr. Sahiba Singh provided valuable ideas about anxiety around the world in different countries.

Some individuals have shared their struggles with anxiety and how they overcame their challenges. They have provided real world validation of the techniques discussed in this book. I am grateful for their honesty and courage in sharing their stories.

The TM Center of Fresno and Certified TM Teacher Michael Neer have provided valuable research evidence regarding the efficacy of Transcendental Meditation. TM, Yoga and other complementary techniques have much to offer the world in the way of relief from anxiety, depression, and the stresses of day-to-day life. I acknowledge their contribution in helping individuals who suffer from anxiety.

TSG

Table of Contents

Detailed Contents

Preface

The prime message of this book is that, if you suffer from anxiety, help is available. Even if you have suffered from anxiety all your life, it can be reduced, and many times may be remedied. It is not something that you have to endure or punish yourself with.

There is much to be gained by giving up your anxiety. A good doctor or therapist or meditation teacher can teach you how to untie that knot of anxiety. That sinking feeling can be stopped. You *can* stand firm and take on the world and the challenges it throws at you. You can be strong, resilient, can overcome and thrive. You can manage your interaction with the world better by knowing more about your world—both outer and inner.

The subject of anxiety is both deceptively simple and yet complex. It can range from the mild jitters everyone feels before an important introduction to the terror of a phobia or a panic attack. Other anxiety states may lead to paralyzing indecision or cause purposeless actions such as the excessive washing of hands in a fantasied attempt to wash away the sin of some errant thought.

There are, in fact, a number of different anxiety disorders with varying symptoms and distinct manifestations.

My goal in this book is to provide you with a better understanding of anxiety—what it is and how it can be treated. This will allow you to communicate better with your health professional about what steps can be taken to reduce anxiety in your life.

Anxiety can be caused by an array of different reasons. The reasons can be medical, psychological, or social in nature. I also like to think that there is also a spiritual component to many of our anxieties. Therefore spirituality, and its role in decreasing anxiety, is also given some mention.

There is a lot of misunderstanding about anxiety. Sometimes people are nervous about their performance—in sports, in school, at work—and, within limits, this anxiety can be good. And then there is the other kind of anxiety that has become detached from the original cause and continues to act in an apparently random manner leading to dysfunction at home, at work and in our social lives. This type of anxiety is the bad kind of anxiety that we need to ward off and get treatment for when it starts interfering in our lives.

I have tried to make this book user-friendly by using illustrations and diagrams and avoiding jargon wherever possible. Some topics may seem out of place or only obliquely related. Such meanderings have the potential for providing unique insights and are therefore included. Sometimes, I have gone into more detail than perhaps is warranted. I felt I needed to elucidate that there is a substrate of logic to all treatments no matter how esoteric they may seem.

The individual chapters can be read as stand-alone chapters in any order of interest. The dots all connect at the end and no one set sequence is better than another. So feel free to jump around in the book. Some pages are provided at the end of the book for your personal notes.

A few sections may be too technical for the average reader but are included for the sake of completeness. I have tried to honor the intelligence of the average reader. Most individuals, I believe, are able to understand the rationale behind things of science and intuition.

This book can be useful for both the lay person and the professional who provides treatment for anxiety. This book is, in fact, addressing three types of readers: the person with anxiety symptoms, the casual reader, and, in the technical sections, the clinician who is involved in providing treatment. The pronoun he or she has been used interchangeably as the discussion is often equally applicable to either gender.

It is my earnest hope that this information is useful for those who seek relief from anxiety and is also useful for those who want to help others with anxiety symptoms. I congratulate you on taking this initiative and wish you much success with your efforts to make that change for yourself and for others.

TSG

Chapter 1

If You Read Nothing Else

If you read nothing else, reading this chapter will give you an overview of what anxiety is and what the different treatment options are.

This figure depicts the core elements of anxiety.

Fear of Harm

Fear of
Rejection

Self Doubt
About
Competence

CORE FEARS IN ANXIETY

These are a fear of harm to self or loved ones, a fear of being rejected, or of being unable to cope with the challenges of one's life due to a perceived lack of competence.

If one or more of these fears is in excess, the resultant state of restlessness is called anxiety. If anxiety is above the normal range, or if it lasts for a duration longer than is considered normal, it is called an anxiety disorder.

The drive and will to exist and not perish is the driving force behind all of life's movement. All of our fears including our desires to be found acceptable, competent and desirable are ultimately linked to this drive and desire for survival.

The average person does not want to be rejected or to be found wanting or deficient in any way. An excess of such concerns however becomes the breeding ground for anxiety.

The intensity of the symptoms can vary from the mild jitters to a disabling turmoil that paralyzes the ability to get anything done.

Physical symptoms are common in high anxiety states. These may include symptoms such as headaches, body aches, indigestion, insomnia, or palpitations. A person in high anxiety may also perspire excessively, or be afflicted with tremulous hands. A more subtle sign may be yawning, fullness of the head, or a tingling skin sensation called paresthesia. Paresthesia due to anxiety is usually caused by unconscious hyperventilation on the part of the person.

The person may seek an appointment with the family doctor for these physical symptoms; it is only upon a more detailed review that the issue of underlying anxiety comes to light.

Next, we will take a brief look at the different levels of anxiety. The levels can vary from mild to moderate to severe anxiety. The key difference between them is the number of symptoms and the level of dysfunction that is caused.

Table 1:   Levels of Anxiety

LEVEL OF ANXIETY	SYMPTOMS	DYSFUNCTION
MILD	A FEW IF ANY PHYSICAL SYMPTOMS; VAGUE SENSE OF UNEASE, DISTRACTIBILITY	MILD DYSFUNCTION IN DAY TO DAY LIFE
MODERATE	SEVERAL SYMPTOMS SUCH AS PERSPIRATION, FAST HEART RATE,DYSPEPSIA, INSMONIA	SIGNIFICANT INTERFERENCE WITH DAY TO DAY LIFE, INTERFERES WITH JOB, HOME LIFE
SEVERE	SIGNIFICANT DISTRESS IN MEETING PEOPLE; FINISHING TASKS	MAYBE UNABLE TO SUSTAIN OCCUPATIONAL ROLE AND RELATIONSHIPS

Anxiety can be graded in terms of severity as mild, moderate or severe. The difference is basically in the number of physical and psychological symptoms and the accompanying level of dysfunction. The greater the number of symptoms and greater the dysfunction, the more severe the degree of anxiety is deemed to be.

Your First Consultation

As a General Rule
Medical Conditions should be ruled
out before diagnosing any
Psychiatric Condition

Your first source when seeking help for anxiety should be your family doctor, who is also called your primary care provider.

He or she can look for any medical causes of anxiety by reviewing your medical history, your symptoms, and doing a full physical examination. Sometimes, if indicated, special laboratory tests or investigations may also ordered. .

This initial medical consultation is necessary so that we are not treating the superficial anxiety symptoms of a serious underlying medical disorder that may otherwise go unrecognized and untreated. The treatment itself in such states is likely to ineffective if there is an underlying untreated medical illness.

If there *is* a medical issue that is causing the symptoms, it should be effectively treated. When the medical condition improves, the anxiety symptoms related to it also improve. .

Case History: Jane is a 34-year-old married mother of two. She has been jittery and is unable to keep herself calm during the day. She is often worried about problems that don't exist and finds her hands shaking when going about her day. At night, she tosses and turns and has a hard time slowing her mind and falling asleep. She finds heat unbearable and prefers the thermostat to be set at a lower temperature than the rest of the family. She is perplexed and has been losing weight. She thinks she definitely needs help in getting to sleep and goes to her doctor for sleeping pills. He takes a careful history, finds that Janet also has a small lump in front of her throat, and orders a thyroid panel to rule out excessive thyroid hormone levels. The results come back indicating high thyroid levels with elevated free thyroxine levels (FT4) and a suppressed thyroid stimulating hormone (TSH) level confirming his suspicions of a state of hyperthyroidism.

Janet receives treatment for her condition and in a few months, her thyroid functioning returns to a normal range— along with a resolution of her anxiety symptoms!

Diagram: Medical Illness and Anxiety

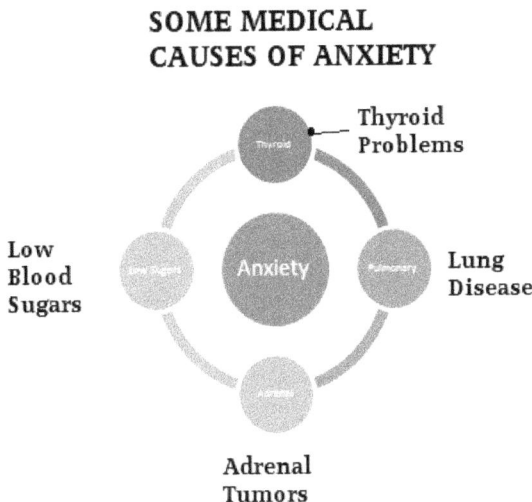

SOME MEDICAL
CAUSES OF ANXIETY

Thyroid
Problems

Low
Blood
Sugars

Anxiety

Lung
Disease

Adrenal
Tumors

What To Say To The Medical Doctor:

When visiting your primary care provider, it is important to be straightforward and direct and come out and say, "Doc, I am having problems with anxiety."

Ask the doctor if he or she can rule out any medical problems that can cause the anxiety that you are experiencing. He or she will consider you enlightened and will honor your wish and provide you a full examination. If he does not, you should consider getting another doctor.

Ask your doctor also if any of the medications you have been prescribed could cause your anxiety symptoms. If you are taking any over the counter medications, this is the time to reveal these as well.

Let the doctor know of these and enquire if any of them could be causing the anxiety.

And if you have been playing doctor and trying to self-medicate by using alcohol or illicit drugs on an episodic or regular basis you should let the doctor know this as well. Depending on the specifics, the intermittent withdrawal or intoxication could be contributing to and exacerbating your baseline anxiety state. You may first need to be detoxified in a safe manner from any alcohol or substance dependence to gauge the true level of your anxiety symptoms.

Do not worry excessively about detox. Detoxification is relatively painless and straightforward in most cases. Abstinence from alcohol or any illicit substances will become the first step towards recovery from your underlying anxiety problem.

Most family doctors have learned about psychiatric symptoms of anxiety and depression at their medical school and are very comfortable listening to these issues. Many are also comfortable prescribing medications to treat anxiety and depressive disorders. Mental health care for the most part is delivered by primary care doctors in their offices with gentle support, guidance and medication.

When medical issues and medication have been ruled out as a cause of your anxiety, ask the doctor what your other treatment options are. You may be pleasantly surprised.

Review Of Treatment Options:

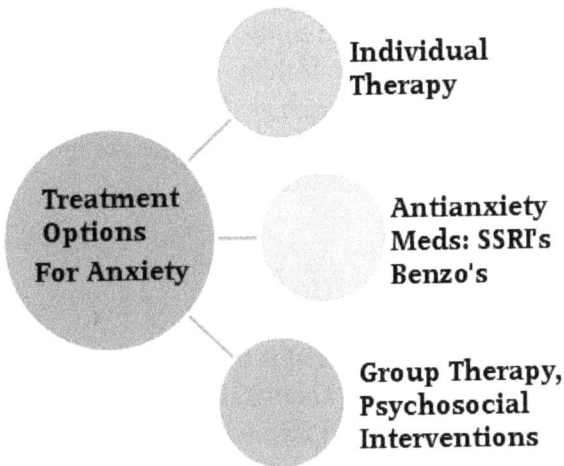

Individual Therapy

Treatment Options For Anxiety

Antianxiety Meds: SSRI's Benzo's

Group Therapy, Psychosocial Interventions

a) If there are no medical issues or medication issues, and *if the anxiety is mild to low moderate*, it may be appropriate to try psychotherapy alone and make some lifestyle changes.

b) *If the anxiety is moderate to severe* and is causing critical dysfunction, it is customary to use both medications and psychotherapy in addition to recommending lifestyle changes.

c) Group therapy, biofeedback, and complimentary techniques can be added to all the other techniques for reducing anxiety symptoms.

Let your treating clinician know if you have been treated for anxiety with any medication in the past and also if the medication worked well or only partially. It may have been the case that you were not treated with the medication at an optimum dose for the optimum duration of six to eight weeks. Upon reviewing the history of "treatment refractory" patients, this has been found to be the most common cause of failed trials of medication in the past. Instead of recreating the wheel, the medication that has worked in the past can be prescribed to save time and suffering and the dose optimized for an optimum duration. If there were sideeffects, different medications should be chosen as there are a wide number of equally effective medications. Well, some are more effective than others but they all do work.

Referral To A Psychiatrist

A Board Certified Psychiatrist is the most qualified person to treat anxiety and other psychiatric disorders. He is able to rule out medical causes, is well trained in psychopharmacology, and has a broad background in general pharmacology and the medical sciences. He or she is also qualified to provide psychotherapy and can provide it or defer it to a trained psychotherapist familiar to him or her. If your family doctor does not wish to prescribe antianxiety medication, he may refer you to a psychiatrist in the area in whom there is confidence based on previous referrals. Most family doctors have a network of specialists who they work with and know which specialists are good in their particular specialty.

What Family Members Can Do For The Anxious Person

If you are a family member or a friend of the person suffering from anxiety, you can help by providing your support, a sympathetic ear, and a nonjudgmental attitude. Remember that excessive anxiety is not a sign of weakness or cowardice. It is often a treatable clinical condition that may develop in any person. It is merely the product of the unique life conditions of the individual. Your friend or family member deserves our sympathy and support and none of the scorn.

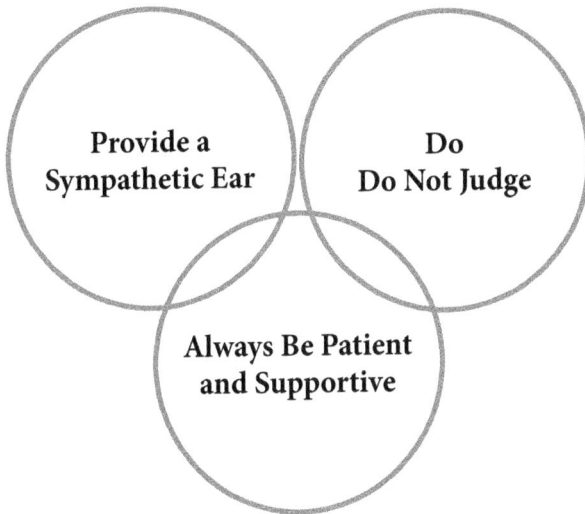

Provide a Sympathetic Ear

Do Do Not Judge

Always Be Patient and Supportive

It is good to remind the anxious person that they are not alone in their struggle, tell them that research indicates that most individuals with anxiety do get better over time on their own and with help. There are millions of people around the world who suffer from anxiety issues, some of them famous and very successful in their careers and personal lives.

The suffering can be curtailed and shortened further with help from a professional who is good at treating anxiety related issues. Such a professional can come from any of the following types of clinicians: The Family Doctor, Psychiatrist, Psychologist, Licensed Clinical Social Worker, Marriage and Family therapist, recreational therapist, priests and pastors from any organized religion.

A Word About Self-Help And Self-Improvement

Self-help and self-improvement is a big movement in the modern culture and many individuals seek enlightenment and betterment of their lives even if they are functioning fairly well.

The techniques used by acolytes of this movement can also help the person suffering from anxiety related difficulties.

There are often weekend conferences and retreats that are maybe worth looking into where much therapeutic work and healing may occur. Some of these retreats can focus on specific issues such as getting over a divorce or relationship, finding greater religious meaning in one's life, meditation camps, life meaning search retreats etc. It is recommended that a person who is acutely anxious avoid such stressful retreats but those who are able to tolerate them should look into these as they may derive significant benefits from such workshops.

Other self-help techniques may include adopting a healthier lifestyle by getting an adequate amount of rest, sleep and exercise. Many find it useful to keep a personal diary and engage in quiet contemplation to sort out their thoughts. At other times, getting away from an abusive or dysfunctional relationship is the most helpful step that one can take for regaining peace of mind.

Quiet contemplation and meditation can yield life changing insights. Insight is like a lightening flash in a dark night of anxiety that can illumine the surroundings and show us the path we need to take. Education through reading on the subject along with patient introspection can yield these insights and higher truths to the diligent person as well. It can happen all at once or gradually grow on you.

Shielding Against Anxiety

For the anxious person, worries can seem like the proverbial rain drops that keep falling. It is useful therefore to have an umbrella of ideas that can give you shelter during such times.

Listed below are some first steps the person with anxiety can consider for obtaining relief. If followed, they have the potential of offering immediate benefits.

- Get Support from Friends and Family: It is helpful to confide in someone who you trust about your anxieties and difficulties. They can offer you support, love and encouragement. They may know a great doctor or therapist and can guide you to them if the condition is severe. You may perhaps find they have had to deal with anxieties similar to yours in their own life making them possible sources for advice and mentorship. They may even offer you advice that will save you a lot of trouble. Don't be afraid to ask for help if you are feeling overwhelmed and need help. Knowing that there is someone that understands even if they cannot help much is useful for lessening anxiety and sense of isolation that it can impose.

- Avoid Erroneous Thinking: Make it a rule for yourself to avoid the following errors of thinking, or what are called cognitive distortions. These are catastrophizing, maximizing, minimizing, personalizing, using a mental filter, and not giving yourself enough credit. These are further explained below.

- Catastrophizing: Thinking the worst is going to happen based on limited data, or the sky is falling syndrome.

- Maximizing: Exaggerating any minor setbacks.

- Minimizing: Underemphasizing positive signs of success.

- Personalizing: Thinking that you are responsible for how someone is behaving or reacting (it may be a scowl or a frown due to any number of other factors).

- Using a mental filter: Disregarding any positive signs and only picking up negative signs in a situation.

- Not giving yourself credit for your past successes in overcoming difficulties. Remember you have skills and strengths to overcome any problem that may come your way.

- Consider joining a local chapter of an Anxiety Disorder Support Group if one exists in your community.

- Check out the local library or the internet for further information.

- Avoid alcohol or illicit substances.

- Avoid excessive use of coffee, tea, and other caffeinated beverages. Be careful to also avoid certain "energy drinks" that contain guarana and other stimulating compounds. These can leave you wired, fidgety, high strung, and anxious.

- If you take any stimulating medication, such as Adderall, or Ritalin for ADHD, or stimulating medications for asthma, check with your doctor as these could be the cause of your anxiety.

- One sure way to know if the medication is the cause of your anxiety is to make a note of your anxiety level in the hour or two after taking the medication when blood levels are rising. If you notice a distinct increase in your anxiety subsequent to taking the medication, you have your answer and should seek an alternative medication from your doctor that does not cause anxiety.

- Setting of a regular sleep pattern and sticking to it can help to reduce anxiety symptoms. This is seriously an important step as studies show that a significant cause of stress in modern life is the lack of sleep. People in industrialized cities and countries are insomniacs by nature and are chronically sleep deprived. Though 'advanced' technologically, they are backward when it comes to the adoption of healthy and sane sleeping habits. An adequate amount of sleep helps boost your coping ability physically and mentally.

- Some over the counter (OTC) remedies for sleep such as diphenhydramine (Benadryl), or valerian- and melatonin-containing compounds (MidNite) may facilitate your sleep onset. Follow the directions and precautions listed for these over the counter compounds. Do not take diphenhydramine if you are over 55, have problems with constipation, urinary retention, or narrow angle glaucoma.

- To cope with stress, start an exercise program. You should ask your doctor when you go to see him or her, if you are healthy enough to begin a light to moderate exercise program. Simple exercises such as walking, a few pushups, and sit-ups, should be started slowly and built up gradually over a 3 to 4 week period. Intermittent exercise through the day may be more helpful than one lengthy exercise session. Exercise, in any form and for however long, is better than no exercise.

- Exercise is therapeutic not only for anxiety but has been proven to help with depression as well. A good workout wherein you break sweat is almost incompatible with anxiety.

- Gardening and Cleaning: Sometimes hidden exercise, such as gardening or cleaning up around the house, or garage or barn, is more acceptable to some individuals. Apart from the exercise benefits, many folks find something deeply rejuvenating and satisfying about gardening, organizing, and cleaning activities.

- If you are one of those who hate formal exercise, you would do well to make a list of tasks around the house that need doing and devote half an hour to an hour every day to this form of "exercise" disguised as chores.

- Meditation: If you are willing to try meditation, you may experience significant benefits in many spheres of your life aside from the lessening of anxiety and worries. As one example, research has shown that Transcendental Meditation (TM) is twice as effective at reducing anxiety than most other meditation techniques.

- However, you don't have to wed yourself to any particular technique and should feel free to try one, or more than one of the techniques available. Keep using what works for your own needs.

- Take Up Martial Arts: Some individuals who have been the victim of physical violence find increased confidence and a decrease of anxiety by taking up martial arts. As they get better in self-defense, it enhances their sense of security and decreases their sense of vulnerability. In addition, the physicality of the martial arts training provides exercise which decreases anxiety and depression by a separate mechanism.

- When learning self-defense, it is important to remember that these are self-defense classes and not intended to wage vengeance or launch an assault on another person.

- Herbs: Some over the counter herbal products such as Valerian, St. John's Wort, Passion flower and chamomile have been found to be helpful for anxiety. They are widely used in Europe and other countries to treat anxiety and depressive symptoms.

- Be cautious with the herbal preparation Kava as it has been associated with some reports of liver toxicity and long-term use has been associated with a form of dermatitis.

- Herbal products are generally safe but may have interactions with other medications. It is wise to check with your doctor before starting these agents. Most notably, St. John's Wort should not be combined with the antidepressant belonging to the monoamine oxidase inhibitor (MAOI). Passionflower preparations should be avoided with Selective Serotonin Reuptake Inhibitors (SSRI's).

- Imagining the Worst-Case Scenario

In this intervention, with the help of a friend or a therapist, you can discuss the worst-case scenario for your anxious fears. You are asked to go over the scenario and add any other details that may come to you. After repeating this a few times, most people begin to realize the absurdity of some of their fears. They find that, even in the worst-case scenarios, they will have options and will not be as helpless as they assumed. This has the overall effect of lowering the anxiety levels.

- Worrying Well: In this technique, you undertake the following steps.

List the anxieties and fears that you have and

1. Make a concrete plan, with as much detail as possible, to address the concerns.

2. Make plans for a contingency wherein your plan falters or falls through.

3. Once you have planned for any contingency that might come up, you will not be constantly distracted by possible negative outcomes. This is because you have already deliberated on the problem and have made a plan to counter any adverse situation that may present itself. When you have plan A, B, C in place, you are much less likely to be surprised. Being psychologically prepared to deal with any eventuality helps to decrease your anxiety.

Factors That Protect Against Anxiety

- The following factors help to decrease the risk of having an anxiety disorder. When one or more of these elements exist in your life, you are much less likely to fall prey to any type of mental illness in general. These protective elements are:

- A supportive spouse or partner

- A good friend who is willing to listen and offer a comforting word or support without being judgmental

- Regular engagement in activities that activate the vagus nerve such as laughing, singing, whistling and humming.

- Strong faith and spiritual leanings

- Regular reading of spiritual texts

- Regular outdoor activities and exercise; exercise can take a simple form such as walking

- Gardening of any sort

- Getting between 6 and 8 hours of sleep every night

- Taking regular vacations, even if only for 2 to 3 days

- Cutting down on multitasking

- Having a dog or another pet

- Good physical health and a balanced diet

- Work that one finds meaningful

- Absence of alcohol or substance abuse problems

Benefits Of Treating Anxiety

1. Reduced Risk of Physical Disease: Excessive anxiety can lead to the development of physical disease and illness. Reducing anxiety protects against this risk.

2. Improved Work Performance: By reducing anxiety, you will enhance your performance at work and in your social sphere. You will improve your sleep and may reduce the need for medications for any medical illnesses caused by anxiety.

3. Enhanced Quality of Life for Yourself and Family: Your enhanced quality of life will also enhance the

quality of life of your family members. When you realize that your happiness and freedom from anxiety determines the level of happiness your children and spouse, you are much more likely to do whatever it takes to get better. You may even take up the exercise and the healthy lifestyle that you were too busy to pay attention to before.

4. Reduced risk of depression: By reducing your anxiety, your risk of depression will also be reduced significantly.

5. Reduced risk of substance abuse: When there is less anxiety, there will be no need to self-medicate for high anxiety symptoms with alcohol or illicit substances.

Chapter 2

A Look at Good and Bad Anxiety

Anxiety can have both positive and negative effects. This chapter will look at both of these. We will start by looking at the positive effects first.

"Good" Anxiety

You might wonder if the idea of "good anxiety" is an oxymoron i.e., an inherently contradictory statement. The truth is that there indeed is such a thing as good anxiety.

The above picture is of a player poised to hit the ball out of the ballpark. He appears tense and anxious but his anxiety is priming him for the best possible swing at the ball. Another scenario is a US president delivering the state of the union address when he nervously finds that the teleprompter on which his speech is loaded is not working. The president goes on, however, despite some initial anxiety, to give a resounding and eloquent speech that closes to the thunderous applause of both the houses.

Both of these are real life examples of anxiety that was mobilized to bring out the best in both the individuals.

This controlled anxiety was good; this is the kind of anxiety that we want to own and use as needed.

Perhaps you have experienced such a mix of anxiety and preparation that brought out the best in you. If you have, then you have just experienced anxiety that is good, anxiety that is redeeming.

This anxiety heightens our awareness, sharpens our senses, and hones our reflexes. A small dose of such anxiety increases the chance of an optimal performance. It is especially helpful when a job requires concentration, focus, and diligence. This good kind of anxiety helps us to be punctual for our appointments and makes the doctors and nurses pay attention to being meticulous with medical procedures.

It is also a good kind of anxiety that makes us conscientious about what we do and how we affect other people.

Our anxiety causes us to be careful about avoiding harm or giving offense to anyone. Such concerns about civic propriety and a healthy anxiety about doing the right thing is, thus, the fulcrum of a civilized and humane society.

Anxiety also drives our curiosity. In our remote semi-simian past, anxiety sparked our curiosity about clouds that thundered and the lightning they released and how that made fire. Through curiosity, we learned to use fire, and keep ourselves warm during cold nights.

This anxiety-driven instinct to explore has led to our learning more and more about our environment. As TS Eliot remarked, anxiety truly has been the handmaiden of creativity. Consequently, in a gradual arc over the eons, we have become the dominant species on Earth and in control of the fate of all other species.

On a philosophical level, our essential apprehension and unease, which some call existential anxiety, makes us seek a greater meaning in life. Our existential anxiety has driven our desire to make the world a better place through social reform, social activism, and through the different spiritual traditions.

The framers of the constitution of many different nations have been ethical, conscientious, and, some would argue, anxious men and women who have striven to create a more perfect society for the common good.

So you see, anxiety in small, manageable amounts can be a very good thing. Such anxiety is not overwhelming or disabling. It helps us perform better at our tasks and helps us create a better life for ourselves and those around us.

Next, we will look at a less desirable side of anxiety—when it has begun to cause problems.

Bad Anxiety

This picture is drawn to depict a woman in the grip of disabling anxiety. She exhibits a blunted and numbed emotional expression, a frightened look, and a thousand mile stare that looks through you. This is found in some patients who have Post Traumatic Stress Disorder (PTSD).

The trauma that generates such PTSD is usually a life-threatening event during which the person felt a loss of control over their destiny. This scary situation often comes along with fears of losing life or suffering grievous bodily injury. PTSD does not develop in every such situation but, when it does, it causes much emotional turmoil and distress. The person often finds it hard to carry on life as before. Normal relationships may be hard to sustain due to the social isolation such patients desire and the emotional disconnection and numbing that occurs. Those who suffer from severe PTSD may also find it difficult to hold down a job. The topic of PTSD will be discussed in more detail later but is cited here to demonstrate a type of anxiety that is dysfunctional or bad.

Other types of anxiety disorders could also have been used as they also cause dysfunction. So in a nutshell, we can say that bad anxiety is that level of anxiety that causes dysfunction. Dysfunction, however small, therefore, is the litmus test for determining whether an anxiety is good or bad. Any anxiety that is bad *can* be treated to decrease the symptoms and dysfunction.

The Fight Or Flight Response

The phrase "fight or flight" is well known and most people at some time or another have heard it. It was originally used in 1932 by Professor Walter Cannon MD of the Harvard Medical School Physiology Department. He used it to describe an acute response that he observed in animals that were exposed to a potential attack or threat to their life.

This fight or flight response is associated with the release of adrenaline-like compounds epinephrine and norepinephrine from the adrenal medulla. This chemical flooding of the bloodstream with stimulating compounds causes an increase in heart rate, increased flow to the large muscle groups, dilation of the pupils, and many other changes that prime the animal for a fight to the death if needed or an energetic attempt at flight to escape the perilous situation.

Humans are also animals, mammals to be more specific, and exhibit a similar response to life threatening situations. Such physiological responses to acute dangers may occur in any of the number of hazardous occupations. Some of these include military service, employment as a firefighter, or employment as a law enforcement officer. Needless to say, it can also occur in anyone who has been the victim of a violent crime.

Stress And Its Relationship To Anxiety Disorders

Both realistic worries and anxiety tend to increase the levels of stress. When anxiety or fear is high, the level of the stress hormone cortisone surges, the secretion of acid in the stomach increases, and our bodies get primed for the fight or flight reaction.

In the course of a normal day, stress, if it occurs, is usually short-lived and the situation is resolved one way or the other. In the case of an anxiety disorder, however, the stress lasts for an unnaturally long periods. This sustained stress, leading to a flight or fight mode of existence, can have devastating effects on both the physical and emotional health of a person.

Hans Selye, a scientist renowned for his work on stress, showed that stress generated by any disturbing event manifested itself in the animal by a swelling of the adrenal gland, an atrophy of the thymus gland (involved in immune function), and by the eruption of duodenal and gastric ulcers from increased acid production. These bodily reactions are mirrored in human beings who are under high levels of stress. They also have elevated levels of cortisol, develop duodenal ulcers, and may have lowered immunity.

Individuals under stress therefore may be more prone to catching a communicable disease. A lowered immune system may also place them at a higher risk of developing cancer and malignancy. It is a known fact that other diseases with lowered immune function such as HIV infection are associated with the development of various cancers and malignancies.

A high level of stress can also lead to an exacerbation of other mental illnesses such as schizophrenia, bipolar disorder, and depression. It makes sense, therefore, to take steps to lower levels of stress when we can. The various techniques discussed in this book will help towards that end.

By lowering our stress levels, we can preserve and enhance our physical and emotional health while adding years to our lives. The proper management of stress can also help in optimal functioning in our personal lives and in our chosen careers or vocations.

Recognizing Stress

If the fight or flight response is not resolved but becomes a chronic continuous state, even in an attenuated form, it can lead to stress that can manifest as anxiety or a physical ailment. Sometimes it can manifest as both.

Stress in a person is revealed by taut emotional expressions, sweaty palms, tremors, and fidgetiness. It can also manifest as body aches, headaches, occasional sighing, and complaints of dyspepsia, irritable Bowel Syndrome (IBS) and various gastrointestinal complaints.

Emotional turmoil and stress may cause insomnia, distractibility, and an inability to deal with the demands of day to day life.

Stress is also cumulative in nature. This means that stressful events add to each other and, without a resolution of the stressful problem to some extent and without a means of regular discharge through recreational activities, exercise or meditation, the levels of stress rise to toxic levels over time.

Sometimes violent acts, general protests or a high turnover of employees are the tip of an iceberg of stress in an organization. The environment that generates such levels of stress should be examined as there are often simple things that can be done to make the situation less stressful for everyone there.

Sometimes, it is found that a personality disordered person is at the helm of affairs in such an environment. Such a person should be relieved of such a role until the matter is fully investigated.

Individuals can tolerate stress for long periods and may try to hide it, but when it keeps on piling up, at some juncture, physical or emotional illness may emerge without the person being aware that it is due to stress.

A person may think that they have everything under control, but when even a minor stressor is added to this accumulated level of stress, it can become the proverbial straw that breaks the camel's back. A person may think that they are "handling" their anxiety or stress, but at a deeper level their soul can mount a silent revolt.

It can produce physical symptoms that may not have any explanations in medical pathology. A secretary may suddenly be unable to use her hand to take notes and a soldier may not be able to use his right hand to shoot a gun or offer a salute. In official jargon, such stress related anxiety responses are called conversion reactions or conversion disorders.

The body is wiser and the heart is more true to the individual. Human feelings can be denied but cannot be ignored or they will make themselves heard through bodily symptoms.

The first step to healing a person under stress and high anxiety is to provide them with empathy, understanding, and a safe place to decompress and relax. A good doctor or a person who wants to help the individual should obtain a psychosocial history and explore the struggles that the person is waging in their life, struggles he or she has probably not shared at any great length with others. The very telling and the recounting back of their struggles in a sympathetic, sensitive environment can become a therapeutic start to their healing.

Treatment usually involves a logical plan to help in some practical way that makes a difference. It can be in any of the multiple areas that may be causing stress. Allowing a person to tell their story, and recounting back to them with empathy and without judgment what you have heard, will let them know that another person understands what they are struggling with. It will also help in building rapport and collaborating together towards a solution.

Even a small amount of assistance can sometimes make a big difference. Stress is usually caused by fears, abusive relationships, financial distress, occupational problems, and by untreated mental disorders.

Diseases Associated With Stress

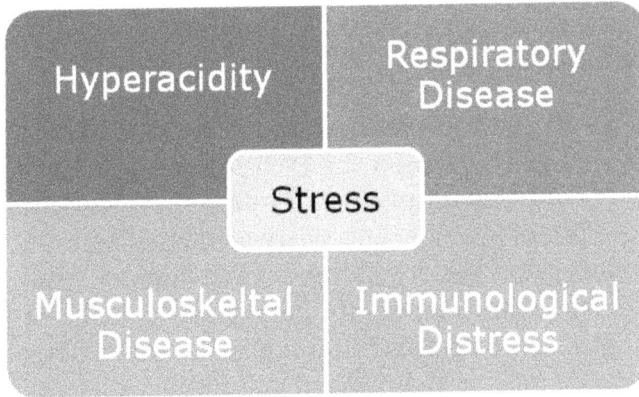

Some notable diseases linked with chronic stress are coronary artery disease, diabetes mellitus, and irritable bowel syndrome. In cases of severe and chronic stress, or severe emotional letdown or emotional shock, a syndrome known as stress cardiomyopathy has also been documented in medical literature—thus the jilted lover may actually die of a "broken heart". Stress cardiomyopathy has also been noted in the overworked nation of Japan where businessmen keep incredibly long work hours and have limited time to decompress or wind down. Stress cardiomyopathy has been given the name Takotsubo Cardiomyopathy and can be a life-threatening condition.

Thus it seems that all work and no play not only makes Jack a dull boy but can also make him very ill and dead.

The following is a list of other medical conditions that are caused by, or exacerbated by, stress and anxiety.

Hypertension
Peptic Ulcer Disease
Asthma
Headaches

Chronic fatigue syndrome
Cystitis
Musculoskeletal Illness

A Scientific Look

The subject of good and bad anxiety has always garnered interest from behavioral scientists.

In this tradition, two psychologists, Robert M. Yerkes and John Dillingham Dodson, in 1908 looked at the effect of anxiety in a systematic manner. They conducted experiments on the effect of incremental anxiety on human performance. They found that anxiety in low to mild amounts enhanced performance but was toxic to performance when the level was high. They reflected their findings in a diagram that has become famous as the Yerkes-Dodson curve. Here is the diagram. You can take a minute to study it.

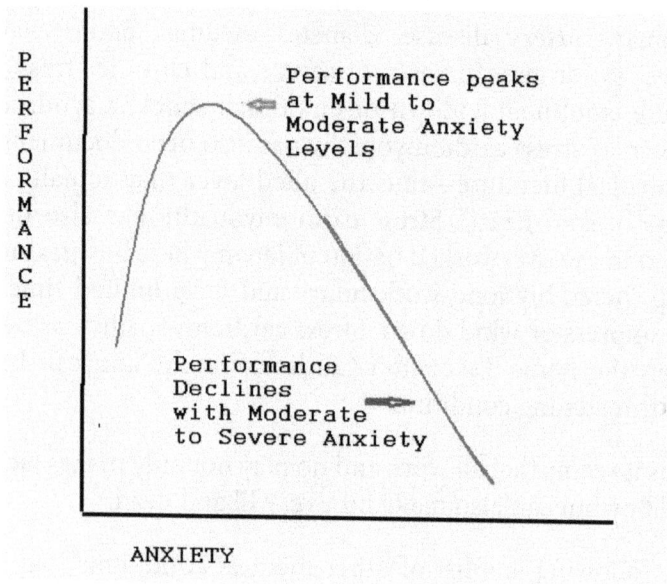

P
E
R
F
O
R
M
A
N
C
E

Performance peaks
⇐ at Mild to
Moderate Anxiety
Levels

Performance
Declines
with Moderate ◄
to Severe Anxiety

ANXIETY

Interpretation of the Yerkes Dodson Diagram:

A mild to moderate amount of anxiety helps performance, as the initial rise of the curve shows. As anxiety increases with the movement of the graph towards the right, the performance curve plummets sharply.

What was it about the increased anxiety that was so harmful to performance? The best guess is that increasing anxiety caused a lack of focus and increased the distractibility of the test subject. Physical symptoms of anxiety such as sweating, palpitations, or tremor, also made the person more aware of their anxiety and more self-conscious. Self-consciousness about the sweating and tremor can increase anxiety further, leading to further symptoms which, in turn, make the person even more self-conscious. At this point, a vicious circle of increasing anxiety reinforcing itself is set in motion.

The classic example of toxic anxiety is a speaker on the stage frozen with stage fright and unable to speak a single word. Another example of toxic anxiety is the athlete who chokes at the crucial moment and is unable to deliver the performance that would otherwise have been second nature to that athlete.

Understanding Of Anxiety By Coaches

This is an interesting aside but the negative effects of anxiety are well understood by good coaches.

In football, when the team kicker is getting ready to kick a crucial field goal, the opposing coach will call a timeout just before the kicker is about to kick. In football lingo, this is done to "ice the kicker".

During the extra time provided by the time out, the coach is counting on self-consciousness and anxiety in the kicker to build to a higher level. The coach understands at a gut level that the extra time will make the kicker more self-conscious and more likely to miss the field goal. The coach is counting on bad anxiety to make his day.

Good coaches also know how to decrease anxiety in their players. They may call an anxious player to the sidelines and talk and banter about a completely irrelevant subject such as a recent barbeque or a favorite restaurant or crack some joke with a player who is anxious. They occupy the extra time provided by the opposing coach with relaxing interactions with their players.

Great coaches simplify the complex and make the players believe they have the tools to overcome any odds that they may be facing. They avoid anxiety by not engaging in finger pointing and not scapegoating one person. They do not allow anxiety to sap the team's strength because they understand well the ill effects of anxiety on morale and performance.

If the coach's team is anxious at half time about losing or their bad performance, a good coach will lessen it by accepting what has gone on but reminding them of their strengths. They will remind them of their prior comebacks, and make them believe that they have the ability to overcome any deficits. They build up morale and team responsibility.

The coach also lessens anxieties about the other team by explaining the play of the other team in simple terms and offering "solutions" to the players even if they have no clue. The act of having a concrete plan using generic strategies serves to lower anxiety in the players.

Giving them a plan, any plan, offers hope and lessens anxiety. He stokes their confidence again and again by reminding them of their fighting spirit and their ability to come back based on their past comebacks.

Great coaches and great generals and great leaders are purveyors of hope and vanquishers of anxiety.

The great coach is in every sense a therapist in the trenches. He can use cognitive behavior strategies, model confidence, give verbal praise, and reinforce by rewards or punishment. He uses whatever is needed to lift his players from certain defeat to a jubilant victory.

Chapter 3

Types of Anxiety Disorders
An Overview

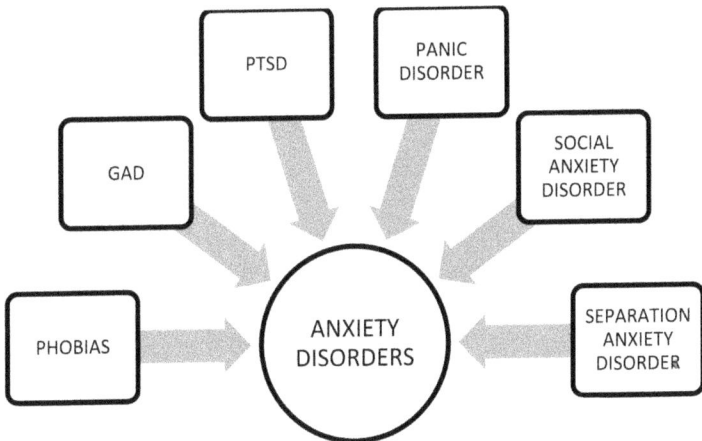

The following types of anxiety disorders are universally recognized across the world.

1. Generalized Anxiety Disorder (GAD): This is a state of heightened anxiety and worry about common things that would not ordinarily bother most people. The individual with GAD worries about any and everything on most days. He or she cannot find assurance from any facts that would be grounds for encouragement to others. The DSM definition of generalized anxiety disorder stipulates that, for a diagnosis of GAD to be made, this dominant and pervasive state of anxiety should have existed for

most days for a duration of six months or more. There is nothing magical about the six months; it is just a number that a group pulled out of thin air and collective experience. A clinician can fudge the duration criteria if they have a gut feeling that the individual otherwise meets the criteria.

2. Obsessive-Compulsive Disorder (OCD): This anxiety disorder is marked by obsessions and compulsions. Obsessions are repetitive thoughts that keep intruding and "popping" into the mind. The person finds them distressing and does not want to have these thoughts but is unable to control them. Compulsions are the behaviors done to make the obsessions or repetitive thoughts go away. The compulsions can get quite complicated and time consuming. They are done with the intention of decreasing the obsessive thoughts but fail to adequately control the unwanted thoughts. The result is that the person can spend increasing amounts of time in ritualistic repetitive behaviors. The obsessive thoughts may be fears of contamination by germs or about not following some rule. To calm these repetitive thoughts, the person may engage in repetitive behaviors such as handwashing. As an example of gravity of the problem, this behavior leads to cracking and bleeding of the skin of the hands in severe cases.

    a) The compulsive behaviors and rituals are repetitive because they are driven by obsessions which are repetitive in nature.

    b) The repetitive handwashing, repeated checking of the locks, or other compulsive behavior in OCD appears irrational and "crazy" to others who do not understand the nature of the illness.

   c) OCD patients, however, are extremely rational and logical in most other things and are not psychotic. The patients are usually intelligent and realize others judge harshly. They may therefore hide their symptoms from others.

   d) This misplaced sense of shame and stigma may also cause some of the patients to avoid seeking treatment from doctors in order to avoid any discussion of their mental lives.

   e) Other patients are often well informed and understand that all doctors are familiar with OCD and do not have a problem understanding the nature of their symptoms.

3. Panic Disorder: This anxiety disorder is marked by recurring surges of anxiety that peak in 1 to 2 minutes and last for 10 to 15 minutes. Panic attacks are distressful to the individual and cause much anguish. The individual may be alarmed and believe that there is a medical cause of their symptoms. They are disappointed when they receive news of a healthy heart and no major medical problems. They may seek second opinions and do not think that they need the services of a psychiatrist. When they do see a psychiatrist, they are pleasantly surprised when symptoms halt with a simple medication regimen.

4. Phobias: This condition is marked by excessive fear or dread of certain objects, animals, or situations. Phobias can develop to anything as evidenced by the long list of phobias cited in the literature. Some of the common examples are phobias of flying, heights, snakes, bugs, spiders and dogs.

5. Social Anxiety Disorder: In this disorder, the individual is excessively self-conscious when in public or around other people. This is related to an almost mortal fear of being judged negatively by others.

6. Separation Anxiety Disorder: In this anxiety disorder, the child or adult may experience acute pangs of anxiety and distress upon being separated from major attachment figures such as their mother or father. Separation Anxiety Disorder may be accompanied by physical symptoms such as a feeling of butterflies in the stomach, weakness, or nausea. Although usually noticed in childhood, it may remain active into late teens and adulthood.

Prevalence Of Anxiety Disorders

In the United States, it is estimated that about 18 percent of the population experience significant problems with anxiety during their lifetime. In about 4 percent of the population, the anxiety disorder is severe.

Prevalence of Anxiety in the General Population

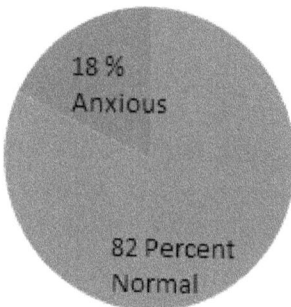

18 %
Anxious

82 Percent
Normal

Severe anxiety can make it difficult for the individual to speak with other people. It can also hamper their job performance and thereby place them at risk of losing their job. If they remain employed, anxiety limits their ability to achieve their full potential in their chosen careers.

The following pie chart shows that about 60 percent of the patients with anxiety disorder patients are women. Although these demographics seem to be drifting towards a more egalitarian representation, women in every culture do manifest anxiety at higher rates than men.

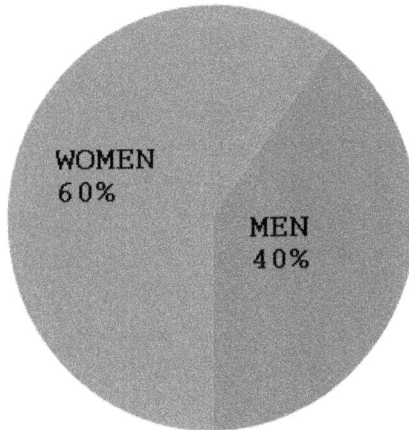

RATIO OF WOMEN TO MEN
WITH HIGH ANXIETY

1. Kessler RC, Chiu WT, Demler O, Walters EE. Prevalence, severity, and comorbidity of twelve-month DSM-IV disorders in the National Comorbidity Survey Replication (NCS-R). *Archives of General Psychiatry*, 2005 Jun; 62(6):617-27.

Learning From Anxiety Around The World

The rates of anxiety vary across the world. Anxiety as a rule is higher in the more technologically advanced nations. For example, the United States has one of the highest rates of anxiety. The rates of anxiety are comparatively lower in European countries, but the lowest rates of anxiety have been found in poor Third World countries such as the Catholic nations of Latin America. Despite the poverty of the masses, it may be that their strong religious faith and close-knit family structures provide protection from high anxiety in their lives.

This surprising calmness of the poor compared to the anxious restlessness in seemingly advanced and prosperous nations has been explained by different theories. One theory states that there are greater stresses and greater demands made upon individuals in the technologically advanced nations. Not the least of these is the exposure to multiple sources of information that keep up the steady stream of breaking bad news around the clock. In addition, there are greater demands to do more in less time and often with diminished resources. Many people go to bed with their smartphones. Some may awaken to check on updates and "statuses" of others. It seems that the more technology intrudes into our lives, the less natural and the more anxiety-prone we tend to become.

The different rates of anxiety in different countries may also be explained by disruptive social events. These may include acts of war, famine, and civil unrest.

It of course does not take an Einstein to figure out that the threat to safety and security is the reason for elevated anxiety rates is such chaotic social situations.

Sometimes, however, there may be a false sense of wellness during a crisis. At such times, people may strangely feel more coherent and clearer in their thoughts due to being collectively organized against a common threat. Following this preternatural calm, there can be a surge of depression and anxiety in the affected populations when reality sets in.

This was noted in the memoirs and tales of British nationals who had survived months of nightly air raids from Nazi Germany. There was also the perceived imminent threat of an all-out invasion of England by the then undefeated German armies. Many of them recall an eerie sense of calm and purpose in the resistance. Churchill of course with his indomitable spirit and cheerleading was another buffer for his countrymen against anxiety in those difficult times. It was only later when going through the rubble that some individuals fell prey to anxiety problems.

The dissolution of the family structure in the more advanced nations is cited as another cause for increased anxiety in westernized nations. There is some merit in this argument as family structure has indeed changed in the west to where single parent homes are becoming more common than dual parent homes.

Some social scientists conjecture that when family structures are disrupted due to any reason- it affects all family members and no one is left unaffected. They echo the thought that the high rates of divorce and broken families may be contributing to higher rates of anxiety and other social ills in society.

Some societies have a high rate of substance abuse and alcohol dependence. When one or more family member in any family is addicted, their dysfunction causes distress and anxiety in all the other family members.

Such homes are also at a higher risk of domestic violence and abuse.

In the final analysis, a slower pace of life with more settled routines seems to be more conducive for the mental, physical, and spiritual health of a population.

If the culture is coherent and stable with intact family structures, it makes for lower rates of anxiety in the population. When the natural state of existence is disturbed, anxieties occur at higher rates.

This is not a call for a Luddite retreat away from progress but an attempt to point out that we must not forget our essential human needs for nurturing that only healthy families can provide. Family friendly nations and organizations provide liberal leave for pregnancy and nurturing of the child. They offer flexible work schedules and allow the parent to take work home to be with their child as long as it does not affect the quality of the work.

In our frenetic rush to do more in the name of progress, we may be giving away more than we stand to gain.

Chapter 4

Causes of Anxiety

This chapter in some ways was the most difficult to write. This is because anxiety can have multiple causes which may interact with each other in complex ways. Having said that, we can categorize the causes into four separate categories. These categories are: biological causes, psychological causes, spiritual causes and social causes. They are depicted interacting with each other in this diagram.

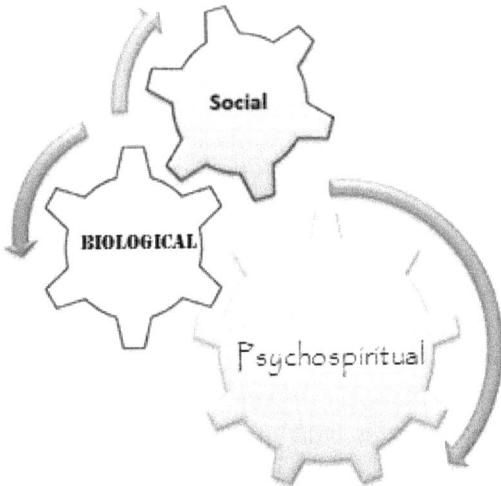

A Model of Anxiety with Spiritual Component

Biological Causes Of Anxiety

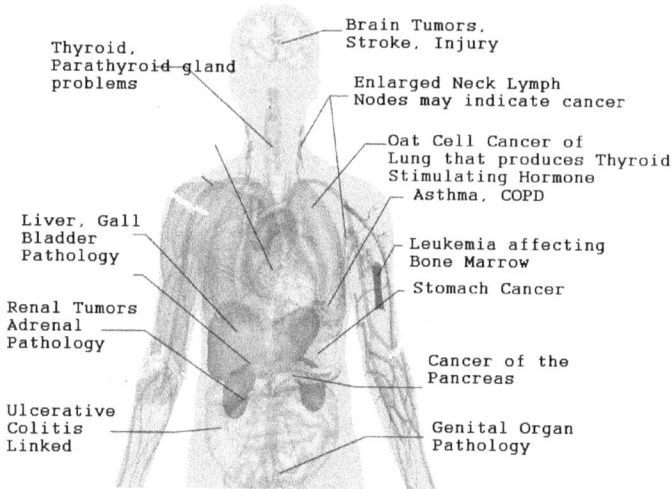

Thyroid, Parathyroid gland problems

Brain Tumors, Stroke, Injury

Enlarged Neck Lymph Nodes may indicate cancer

Oat Cell Cancer of Lung that produces Thyroid Stimulating Hormone

Asthma, COPD

Liver, Gall Bladder Pathology

Leukemia affecting Bone Marrow

Stomach Cancer

Renal Tumors Adrenal Pathology

Cancer of the Pancreas

Ulcerative Colitis Linked

Genital Organ Pathology

Diagram Explanation: *Brain Tumors, strokes and any injury to the brain can affect mentation and emotions. Enlarged neck lymph nodes (Virchow's nodes) may indicate cancer in distant organs which can have psychiatric implications. Leukemia often results in anemia and vulnerability to infections, the use of antineoplastic agents which may have secondary affects resulting in anxiety or depression. Cancer of the pancreas is well known to cause depression with vague and foreboding anxiety. Genital organ pathology may result in hormonal changes that can affect mood and thereby cause anxiety symptoms. Any issues with the genitalia may also affect the person's self-concept and lead to anxiety symptoms. Ulcerative Colitis and Irritable Bowel Syndrome have both been linked with high anxiety states and their resolution is contingent on effectively treating anxiety symptoms. The liver produces many useful compounds the body needs and is also the waste processing unit of the body that detoxifies and metabolizes* *food, drugs and other compounds that we ingest. When the liver is affected, it has a definite effect for the negative on the mentation of the individual and anxiety symptoms may be seen. In severe liver pathology, encephalopathy and delirium may ensue due to elevated ammonia levels. The gall bladder stores and releases bile at opportune times to facilitate absorption of fat soluble vitamins. When the gall bladder is dysfunctional, it may cause malabsorption leading to secondary anxiety and mood symptoms. A tumor of the adrenal glands called pheochromocytoma leads to surges of anxiety that can be misdiagnosed as being due to a panic disorder. Kidney disease can affect formation of blood, production of vitamin D and regulation of electrolyte balance in the blood. Disruption in any of these functions can lead to anxiety symptoms in addition to other complications that require dialysis. The glands in front of the neck are the thyroid and behind the thyroid are four parathyroid glands. If they are overactive or underactive, significant anxiety and mood symptoms can develop.*

Many medical illnesses can therefore cause anxiety in unique ways. By treating these underlying medical illnesses, anxiety symptoms may often resolve on their own without further interventions.

The following is a little bit more detailed discussion of the medical conditions that can cause anxiety.

Hyperthyroidism: In this condition, there is a higher than normal level of thyroid hormones due to overactivity of the thyroid gland. This hormone determines the rate at which the body burns the food that we consume. This is also called the basal metabolic rate (BMR). An elevation of the BMR due to elevated thyroid hormone thyroxine leads to increased heart rate, increased peristalsis, tremors, and anxiety. The increased "burning" of fuel or the food that we consume can also lead to weight loss. This hormone is abused by some individuals trying to lose weight and they can end up with a state of high anxiety as a result of the high levels of thyroid hormone.

Pheochromocytoma: This is a tumor of the adrenal gland. Excessive levels of stimulating epinephrine, norepinephrine, and dopamine are produced by this tumor. These chemicals are normally produced by the adrenal medulla for the flight or fight reaction discussed earlier. When there is a tumor of the adrenal medulla, these chemicals are produced in greater abundance. When they get dumped into the bloodstream at random intervals, it leads to a state of excitation and arousal along with a surge of anxiety. The physical symptoms produced by this excessive load of adrenaline are a fast heart rate, palpitations, tremors, and increased rate of respiration. These physical symptoms, along with the surge of anxiety, can look very similar to a panic attack.

Respiratory Problems: Acute or chronic respiratory problems, such as asthma, emphysema, or chronic bronchitis, may generate respiratory distress and such distress can cause anxiety.

Anemia: Anemia denotes a lower than normal concentration of red blood cells and thereby hemoglobin in the blood stream. Hemoglobin is required to bind oxygen in the lungs and transport it to different cells of the body. It also transports carbon dioxide from the tissues to the lungs for exhalation. When hemoglobin levels are low, the heart must beat faster in order to supply enough oxygen to the different organs and tissues. This acceleration in the heart rate can lead to the person becoming perceptive of their heartbeat. This experience of becoming self-aware of the heartbeat can be associated with anxiety.

Micronutrient deficiencies

Vitamin deficiencies of thiamine, B12, folate, niacin, and possibly vitamin D, have been associated with various psychiatric and physical symptoms. Vegetarian diets may result in B12 deficiency, and certain medications such as phenytoin and isoniazid may induce folate and B6 deficiency. The various malabsorption syndromes due to any cause may contribute to deficiencies of other micronutrients. It is important to be aware of these and provide supplementation when needed. The psychiatric symptoms of micronutrient deficiencies are often ill-defined but may include slowed mentation, depression, paresthesias and anxiety.

Cancer of the pancreas This has been associated with depression and a foreboding sense of anxiety. These symptoms sometimes present themselves months and years before the physical diagnosis of pancreatic cancer is suspected based on physical signs or symptoms.

Deficiency of hormones: Deficiency of hormones, such as estrogen in women or testosterone in men, may lead to anxiety and depressive symptoms.

Brain tumors and strokes: Brain tumors and strokes have been linked with specific anxiety and mood syndromes depending on the area of the brain that is involved. Typically, strokes on the left side of the brain with right sided weakness are associated with depression and anxiety while right sided strokes with left sided weakness may lead to an elevation of mood and irritability. Strokes in the right parietal lobes may lead to unique symptoms of neglect of the left half of the body. It can be made obvious by behaviors such as not shaving the left side of the face because the person does not apprehend and is truly not aware of the existence of the left side.

Hormone-producing tumors: Certain tumors of the lung or other organs can produce abnormal chemical compounds that may have hormone-like effects. This can lead to anxiety symptoms if these hormones stimulate the thyroid gland or cause stimulation of the autonomic nervous system.

Cardiac problems: Many cardiac problems, such as congestive heart failure or arrhythmias, can lead to palpitations, shortness of breath and secondary anxiety symptoms. When the arrhythmias are controlled and the cardiac output is increased, the anxiety symptoms also remit and decrease.

Withdrawal from sedatives or hypnotics: Withdrawal from sedatives is marked by return of the opposite set of symptoms. In the case of withdrawal from sedatives, the opposite symptom of anxiety and excitation is common. This may be marked by perspiration, fast heart rate and anxiety. The opposite of sedate is a state of anxiety and this is what you get in a rebound from sedatives. These withdrawal symptoms can be controlled by offering the original agent or an agent that affects the brain in a similar manner and slowly tapering it off on a daily basis. A comfortable approach for detox is a 20 percent daily reduction of the total dose required to control the initial withdrawal symptoms on the first day.

Withdrawal from alcohol: Alcohol is a molecule (C_2H_5OH) that has a panoply of effects on the brain. Its effects are marked by initial excitation followed by sedation. The brain is affected in multiple ways that are not fully understood. Withdrawal from alcohol is marked by anxiety, tremors, and an increased heart rate amongst other symptoms.

Withdrawal from opiates: Withdrawal from opiates, such as heroin or methadone, may be marked by nausea, increased heart rate, anxiety, sweating, vomiting and diarrhea. Such withdrawal can be uncomfortable but can be safely managed. Extra medical supervision may be needed if there are any serious preexisting medical conditions.

Intoxication with psychedelic agents: Psychedelics have the propensity for producing dissociative states which may generate intense anxiety in individuals.

Intoxication with stimulant drugs: Anything that stimulates can lead to increased heart rate, palpitations and anxiety.

Acute Pain: Any medical condition that causes acute pain or respiratory distress often causes anxiety. Such anxiety is useful in that it makes the individual seek help for a potentially serious medical condition.

Hypoglycemia (Low blood sugar): Low blood sugars are usually caused by a missed meal in the diabetic patient on medications, or due to a miscalculation in the dosage of insulin. The simple solution to hypoglycemic anxiety is to offer fruit juice or glucose paste or sugar in any form. If none of these are available, any type of food will do. The person should be monitored and taken to the hospital as close monitoring may be required if the overdose is due to a long acting insulin. Rare tumors of the pancreas that produce an excess of insulin (insulinoma) can also induce low blood sugar states by the same mechanism.

Pulmonary Embolism: Pulmonary embolism or clots to the lungs can be caused by the existence of a hypercoagulable state of blood. In this state, which is found in some malignancies and cancers, clots may form in the deep veins, break off, and send showers of coagulated blood that find their way to the pulmonary bed of the lungs. Clots may also form when a person is immobile for a long period of time, such as in transcontinental plane flights or when bedridden due to an illness. Pulmonary embolism may lead to sudden chest pain, respiratory distress, anxiety and is a medical emergency.

Pneumothorax: This condition can be spontaneous or can occur after physical trauma and injury. In this situation, air fills the space between the two enveloping sheaths of the lungs—the visceral and parietal pleura. As air fills this potential cavity and makes it real, the ballooning of this space squeezes the lungs and reduces their ability to effectively exchange oxygen and carbon dioxide. This leads to a sense of air hunger and mounting anxiety.

Head injuries: Head injuries are relatively more common than one would think. They can lead to a sense of apprehension and anxiety in the acute phase, and a subsequent syndrome of emotional lability, irritability, and mood instability. In the acute phase, the patient is placed on neurological checks including pupil size and vital signs are monitored (such as the blood pressure, breathing and pulse rates). These checks are done to monitor the development of extra dural or subdural bleeding in the brain. Duramater is the outermost covering of the brain that separates the brain from the interior of the skull. The bleeding outside of the duramater (extradural) or under the duramater (subdural) can lead to increased anxiety, a slowing of the heart rate, the development of neurological signs of brain compression, and later to a decline in the level of alertness. Whenever there is a decline in alertness or an abnormality in the pupils within 24 hours after a head injury, it is a medical emergency and requires surgical intervention to remove the blood clot.

Epilepsy: Epileptic patients may experience anxiety symptoms in between episodes of epileptic attacks and during the prodrome before the epileptic attack.

Dehydration: Dehydration can lead to a sense of feeling faint, and a fast heart rate along with anxiety. Many individuals as they age lose the sensitivity to the sensation of thirst and maybe dehydrated and anxious without being self-aware of this. A urinalysis indicating a high specific gravity, and decreased skin turgor maybe clinical clues to the existence of this problem.

Medications That Can Cause Anxiety

The following medications may cause anxiety.

- Albuterol, and similar B2 agonist inhalers used for asthma

- Stimulants such as methylphenidate (Ritalin, Concerta) or amphetamine salts (Adderall, Vyvanse) used to treat ADHD

- Over the counter or prescribed stimulants used as dietary aids

- Theophylline (Theodor) - used to treat asthma

- Stimulants used in cold medication marketed as decongestants

- Interferon used for treatment of Hepatitis C and other viral infections

- Over the counter herbals that contain caffeine, ephedra, ma huang and other herbals with stimulant effects

- Over the counter decongestants such as Sudafed, nasal vasoconstrictors such as Afrin, Neosynephrine and other such compounds in this class

- Over the Counter diet pills contain stimulants like sibutramine that can cause anxiety, fast heart rate, and palpitations as a side effect.

- Antipsychotics used to treat psychotic illness or mood disorders. These agents include those that block dopamine receptors. Some of these agents are as follows: haloperidol (Haldol), fluphenazine (Prolixin), thiothixene (Navane), trifluperazine (Stelazine), risperidone (Risperdal) and others

The anxiety-generating side effect is called akathisia which literally means the inability to remain still. This side effect can be treated by adding medications such as diphenhydramine (Benadryl), benztropine (Cogentin), or propranolol (Inderal). Sometimes lowering the dose or changing the medication can alleviate this side effect as well.

Psychological Causes Of Anxiety

Learned Behaviors

Incorrect Cognitions

Abusive Relationships

Anxiety Due To Past Abuse

An abusive relationship can eat away like cancer at the self-concept of a person to the point where they may sink into a depression and also become stricken with a sense of shame, self-consciousness, and anxiety. In an abusive relationship, the trauma may be both emotional and physical.

Psychopaths And Anxiety

Living in an abusive situation where one is exploited can be terribly caustic to the psyche and the soul. If the perpetrator of the abuse is a psychopath, the series of lies that are woven around the victim can leave them dazed, confused, and clawing for their sanity.

Many victims of psychopathic exploitation may develop low self-esteem, lose a coherent sense of themselves, and manifest bizarre psychosomatic symptoms and anxiety. They may also lash out in a self-destructive manner due to minor provocations.

Emotional Trauma

This may be caused by a threat to the life of the person, or it may be due to a shock to the person's sense of self-esteem. There may be flashbacks of a traumatic event, nightmares, secondary avoidance phenomenon, and numbing of emotional responses.

Anxiety As A Learned Behavior

Anxiety can be learned and picked up by the child from his or her parents. It has generally been found that anxious children often have an anxious mother or father. Although some of the child's anxiety may be due to anxious genes, the role of social modeling and learning by example from anxious caretakers may be a factor as well. Human beings, especially during childhood but even as adults, continue to learn a great deal of their emotional and social skills from watching parents or other leaders in their environment.

The role of a good parent, and a leader for that matter, is to display confidence, poise, and a constructive attitude towards solving difficulties and problems that may come up. Their equanimity and good humor during a crisis, minor or major, can set the emotional template for competent handling of anxiety in their children.

So, in other words, if the parent handles stressful situations in a calm, confident manner without becoming overwhelmed, the child is more likely to also adopt a similar mode of coping with stress. By treating the anxiety of the parent, many times, the child's anxiety also begins to improve.

Learned anxiety is also prominent in animals as well. As Cesar Milan, the famous "dog whisperer", often explains in problem pet cases, the owner's anxiety is the cause of the dog behaving in a dysfunctional way. As Cesar often states, it is important to project a calm, assertive energy that says you have things under control to decrease the anxiety in the pets and their acting out. The assertive energy is never abusive but patient and diligent in nature.

Although human beings are not dogs, the same principle about learned anxiety applies to human beings as well. It is important for the parent to display a calm confidence that does not get easily flustered and handle obstacles and difficulties with calm and equanimity. For the sake of your family and children, learn to do this even if you don't feel it inside. It will have an eddying effect and the calmness of your family will come back to calm you in return.

Separation In Early Childhood Or Loss Of One Or More Parents

A consistent parent or a consistent caretaker is needed to give the child a sense of stability and security in the world. Attachment theorists have called this object constancy. This is basically the imbibed belief and confidence acquired by the child through their experience with a mother or caretaker who is present when a need arises for them. This is abiding faith that all will be well even though the caretaker is not immediately present.

When this is absent, due to the parent being away or being unavailable, the child may experience anxiety and a lasting sense of vulnerability. This can manifest as generalized anxiety disorder, dependent personality traits, or separation anxiety disorder.

As adults, a strong belief in God can replace this faith of childhood. This succor and support is the great promise of all major religions: a promise that there is a benign, benevolent caretaker who will be there to help them through any calamity that may come up. Faith is a wonderful thing for those who have it. It provides a sense of completeness and a sense of confidence to face any challenges that may come up in the future.

The child also learns to communicate emotions through emotional interactions with the mother, or father or whomever the primary caretaker happens to be. The various games of early childhood such as peekaboo and surprise are games that are present in every culture. They are intuitively engaged in by the mother to see the delight on her child's face every time the mother reappears.

This nurturing instinct must have essential value for the healthy growth of the baby as it appears to have been almost encoded into the human DNA. This exchange of laughter, of smiling, and other emotions in the back-and-forth exchange helps the child to enrich his or her emotional repertoire.

In children who have been orphaned or placed in institutions where this does not occur, the result is a child who is lonely, clingy, and bereft of a sense of security or belonging. He or she may be unable to reciprocate and receive emotions effectively. The child's affect may be blunted, or flat, constricted, or inappropriate, much like a schizophrenic patient.

Not only does this child carry the burden of anxiety and a sense of inadequacy (not being good enough), he also shoulders the burden of social isolation not of his own making. He or she pines for comfort but is unable to elicit or receive it from others effectively.

The social awkwardness can lead to social alienation and further self-consciousness on the part of the child. This can lead to anxiety disorder in childhood and as an adult.

The loss of a parent can cause a deep emptiness that a child may find difficult to fill. The lonely child may seek approval and comfort by being an entertainer, or by being excessively friendly.

Some of the most admired entertainers have been some of the loneliest people and have suffered the loss of a parent, deprivation, and loneliness in their childhood.

Even amidst the adulation and approval from others, they still feel empty, unloved and unredeemed in some way. Some of these actors and entertainers take to using alcohol or drugs.

The fortunate ones may have a supportive aunt or uncle who provides them with unconditional love and regard which can have a protective effect from the absent or noxious parent(s).

Others are intelligent enough as adults to get help for themselves in therapy and through the cultivation of a sincere and supportive network of friends.

Those who survive such childhoods often have great resilience and are successful in their social and personal lives. They have the intelligence to recognize their own dysfunction are able to rise out of any self-destructive behaviors.

Others who have lost a parent in their childhood may take a religious and mystical approach to soothe their emptiness.

Many of the religious leaders in the past have endured the absence of a parent in their early childhood. Perhaps they are reaching out for acceptance from the ultimate parent. Perhaps they found God in a very real form to fill the emotional emptiness of their lives.

Social Causes of Anxiety

Humans are social creatures. We derive meaning for our existence through our relationship with others. When our social life is disrupted, our emotions suffer as well.

The following disruptive social factors may lead to a heightened risk of anxiety symptoms

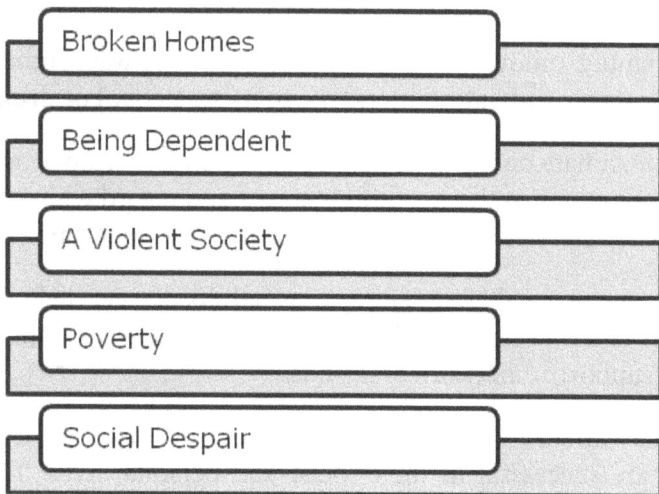

- Broken Homes
- Being Dependent
- A Violent Society
- Poverty
- Social Despair

Broken Homes:

As discussed in the section on anxiety in different countries, in the western cultures, the divorce rate is rising to an all-time high of almost 50 percent and the institution of marriage and the nuclear family is fast becoming just another lifestyle choice.

There is something to be said for the positive effect of intact families. The presence of both parents in a loving relationship with each other and a nurturing relationship with the children provides the crucible for the development of healthy children.

The absence of fathers in the home has been linked in a few cases to higher rates of delinquency and arrests in the children of such homes. Both the mother and father can provide their own type of love, support, and modeling that the children in the family can benefit from.

Sometimes, however, it is better to have a single parent home rather than a home where one of the parents is abusive. In such situations, the children can be raised in a healthy manner by a single parent through support from others and by spending more time with the children.

Lack of a same sex parent for long periods during the earlier years can lead to gender identity issues for some children when they grow up.

Domestic Violence:

Domestic violence causes anxiety for all family members due to obvious reasons. It destroys the idea of faith in a stable and secure mother and father who can provide security for the children. It alienates the two adults in the most intimate of relationships from each other. The abused partner may feel trapped and the abuser may feel guilty and trapped as well. There are often coexisting alcohol and substance abuse problems which generate possibilities of anxiety from intoxication or withdrawal.

Being In A War Zone Or A High Crime Neighborhood:

Exposure to situations that threaten the life and security of any individual will lead to anxiety. If the trauma is severe, the risk of PTSD is higher.

Alcohol Or Substance Abuse Problems In Self Or In A Family Member:

This may lead to a sense of unpredictability and consequent anxiety about the person and the relationship. The substance abuse problems may result in physical or emotional abuse, separations, divorces, or worse.

Being Dependent On Others

Children and the dependent elderly may be at higher risk of anxiety if they have an unreliable caretaker or support source.

Homelessness:

Due to their vulnerability, many homeless individuals become victims of violence, sexual exploitation, and social ills such as alcohol and substance abuse. There is also the risk of exposure to the elements, of going hungry, and the ever-present threat of being imprisoned for minor infractions. Some may even court imprisonment if survival on the streets becomes excessively tenuous or dangerous. Many of the imprisoned are homeless and many homeless individuals are chronically mentally ill.

Unemployment Or Threat Of Unemployment:

The lack of secure employment is a source of great anxiety for many people. The prospective loss of employment can jeopardize the quality of life and sometimes the security of the individual and the family. This threat to the source of livelihood can therefore be extremely threatening and anxiety inducing in an individual

Being A Member Of A Persecuted Minority:

In almost every country, there are sects or subgroups that are set apart by customs and beliefs. They often are scapegoated by majority groups for any ills that may be prevalent in society. Such systemic persecution leads to a state of continued stress that can generate anxiety disorder in the populations of these subgroups. Secondary substance abuse and delinquent behaviors for obtaining illicit substances may also be more common in persecuted groups. Such secondary conduct issues may become further fodder for propaganda against these groups. The civilization or barbarity of any culture, therefore, can often be gauged by the protection provided to its minorities.

Incarcerated Individuals:

Many incarcerated individuals find themselves there for minor crimes and may not be ready for the brutal existence in a jail or prison. Many become victims of violence and some become victims of sexual assault and rape. The shame resulting from this may be tremendous and lead some to suicide. There is also very high risk of individuals becoming infected by blood borne communicable diseases such as hepatitis C, Hepatitis B, HIV, and other illnesses. The high rate of these illnesses among prison populations may be due to sexual activity, the ubiquitous imprinting of tattoos with shared implements, and sharing of needles in some situations. All these risk factors create an atmosphere that breeds anxiety and despair.

Chapter 5

Why Some Are at Higher Risk for Anxiety

When we look at the data, it becomes apparent that the prevalence of anxiety is higher in certain segments of the population. We can learn something useful by taking a look at these groups and examining their unique risk factors.

It is important to remember that not everyone who belongs to a high risk group will develop an anxiety disorder. It only means that they will have to deal with added stressors that may be present in their day to day roles. By being aware of these risk factors, they can take healthy steps to decrease the stress levels in order to avoid the development of an anxiety disorder. Supervisors who deal with such workers can also be more perceptive and refer their workers for help and assistance in due time before they become dysfunctional from stress or anxiety. The supervisors can also be more sympathetic and take steps to improve morale in such working environments.

We will first list the high risk groups and then take a more detailed look at each group will follow. So here are the groups at high risk for development of an anxiety disorder:

- Women in almost all age groups

- Those with a history of childhood abuse of any kind

- Those who have lost a parent in their childhood due to death, divorce, or any other cause

- Homeless individuals
- Those with substance abuse or alcohol abuse related problems
- The disenfranchised and persecuted groups
- Those with acute medical illnesses
- Military personnel from any branch
- Police and Law Enforcement Personnel
- Firefighters
- Workers on acute psychiatric wards
- Workers in Trauma Medicine
- Those in difficult and unhappy relationships
- Those who are incarcerated

Women And Anxiety:

Some of the key risk factors in women that predispose them to anxiety are depicted in the following diagram.

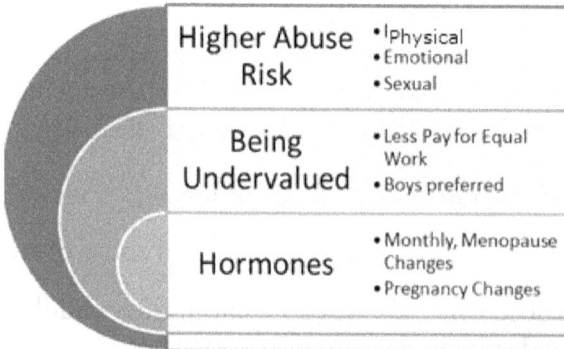

Higher Abuse Risk	• Physical • Emotional • Sexual
Being Undervalued	• Less Pay for Equal Work • Boys preferred
Hormones	• Monthly, Menopause Changes • Pregnancy Changes

RISK FACTORS FOR ANXIETY IN WOMEN

Women in general tend to have higher rates of anxiety than men. This is in part due to a higher incidence of sexual, physical and emotional violence towards them.

Women are also subject to hormonal changes related to pregnancy, the monthly menses and menopause. A combination of these factors is felt to lead to the higher levels of anxiety and higher prevalence of depressive disorders in women.

The Physiology Of Ovulation And Menses:

This is a bit technical, so if you are not inclined, you may skip over this section.

At the beginning of the menstrual cycle, there is a steady rise in estrogen levels leading to the ripening and ovulation of the egg. Subsequently, progesterone levels begin to rise in order to prepare the uterus lining for the egg. As ovulation occurs, the egg travels through the fallopian tube. If fertilization with a sperm cell occurs, the fertilized egg implants itself in the wall of the uterus and progesterone levels begin to rise further in a dramatic manner to ensure the survival of the fertilized egg. If fertilization does not occur, however, the egg is not implanted and the progesterone levels fall steeply, leading to a shedding of the innermost blood-engorged layer of the uterus. This shedding of endometrial lining becomes the monthly menstrual flow.

Premenstrual Syndrome And Anxiety

When the progesterone and the estrogen are rising, there is a sense of well-being in most women, and when these levels fall, there is a corresponding correlation with negative emotions such as anxiety, depression and irritability. When the negative symptoms are severe in some women, it is called late luteal phase dysphoric disorder, per the current nomenclature. In the past, it has also been known as premenstrual syndrome (PMS).

These are serious emotional burdens for some women and should never be referred to in a belittling or condescending manner. They deserve attention as full clinical conditions that may benefit from treatment.

Treatment for the Late Luteal Phase Mood Syndrome or Dysphoric Disorder may involve the use of a SSRI such as fluoxetine (Prozac) for a week to 10 days during the middle of the third week of the menstrual cycle. It can provide relief for many sufferers from this biological syndrome.

Other commonsense measures to help the woman in this difficult period maybe something simple such as a kind word, assistance with some task, or some other loving gesture such as flowers. Any of the stress management techniques can also provide effective relief as well and obviate and eliminate the need for medication.

Dysphoria during this state denotes a subjective mixed state of anxiety, restlessness, and sadness. It may be outwardly marked by isolation, tearfulness, and irritable outbursts.

The wise husband or boyfriend can figure out when the premenstrual phase is due and be extra loving and supportive during this phase to help her get over the few rough days. It can improve the relationship quite a bit. This can be something as simple as assuring her of your love or doing small things that demonstrate this. The premenstrual phase often begins a few days after the full moon in most women.

So although the full moon is the universal sign for romance, the true value of romantic gestures maybe most appreciated a week later when a woman vulnerable to depression caused by a decline in her hormone levels. She will most benefit from the ardor and affections of her suitor at such a time. A kind gesture, an offer of help will go a long way and of course a bouquet of flowers never goes out of style. This will also have the benefit of strengthening their relationship for the future.

Pregnancy And Postpartum Blues

Women also carry the burden and bliss of pregnancy. While there is a definite glow of well-being that pregnancy brings to some women, others are beset with morning sickness, vomiting, and related malaise.

When the baby is born, there are significant stressors such as blood loss, rapid shifts in fluids, and fluctuation of electrolytes. There is also a steep fall in the levels of progesterone that can predispose the mother towards sadness and a feeling of emptiness. In fact, postpartum blues are almost universal in most women and may be marked in some by sadness, restlessness and anxiety. It usually lasts for a day or two and then resolves.

A supportive family member can be a good emotional support for the new mother. They may also offer practical help with caring for the baby and simple activities of daily living that may be an effort for the new mother.

Most women find childbirth and new motherhood to be a positive and happy experience. It is important for family and close friends to provide support to the new mother, and offer to help her in whatever way is needed.

Postpartum Depression And Post-Partum Psychosis

Very infrequently, a more serious condition called postpartum depression and postpartum psychosis can develop. This appears to be a totally separate process from the post-partum blues discussed earlier and may have a different mechanism whereby it gets triggered. Oftentimes, there is a family history of a similar episode in the mother of the new mother. The behavior of the mother in the throes of postpartum psychosis or postpartum depression can be unpredictable. A psychiatric hospitalization is almost mandatory in such situations.

There is some literature to suggest that the postpartum psychosis is a harbinger of schizophrenia for some women. Some reports also indicate a genetic vulnerability to the development of postpartum depression as evidenced by a similar condition having appeared in the postpartum state of other relatives.

If such a history is present or if the mother has gone through a postpartum depression in a previous pregnancy, the use of antidepressants in the last two months of her pregnancy can be considered to prevent the onset of postpartum depression.

Risk To Child From Psychosis In The Mother

During the state of postpartum depression or postpartum psychosis, there is a significant risk to the child if the mother is psychotic. The baby should not be left alone with her during such states.

Breastfeeding And Emotional Health

Breastfeeding usually has a positive effect on the emotional state of the mother and is also tremendously helpful for the newborn. The child receives colostrum in the beginning which provides passive immunity from many of the prevailing illnesses while his or own immune symptom becomes more mature. The mother also benefits from the nurturing and bonding with the baby and also due to the hormones released during breastfeeding. The prolactin is released for continued production of milk and oxytocin is released for the letdown of the milk. Both of these hormones have been found to have a positive and beneficial effect on the emotional health of the mother. Breastfeeding is thus not only a good thing for the newborn but also for the new mother due to the health promoting effects of prolactin and oxytocin.

Health Effects Of Pregnancy And Anxiety

Women run the risk of anemia due to blood loss at childbirth and due to the monthly menstrual flow. Anemia and some of the micronutrient deficiencies associated with anemia, such as low iron, folate and B12 levels, can also appear. Low levels of some of these nutrients have been correlated with anxiety and mood symptoms. It is useful therefore to check for blood levels of these agents and provide supplementation when indicated by a low level.

Raising Of Newborns And Stress For Women

Having to be the primary caretaker of a fragile newborn while the new mother is trying to recover herself can be difficult. She may be sleep deprived due to multiple awakenings by the baby during all hours of the day and night. The timetable for feeding can vary to provide on demand feeding that is recommended. Every act of toileting or bathing the baby and concern about the safety of the baby can be a constant stressor. The mother is expected to always be loving and nurturing and any irritation may be perceived as a fault by others. This may lead to confusion in the mother and a sense of guilt may crop up. All of these factors work on the mind of the new mother and it is at such times that the wisdom and experience of an older female family member who has gone through this can be of immense help.

In later years, the job of raising children can pose other challenges and stresses. As always, it makes it much better and much easier if the spouse is supportive, kind and understanding. A supportive husband who shares the tasks of child rearing is a great blessing for her.

Interesting Turnaround At Menopause

At the other end of her reproductive years, a woman must go through menopause. At this juncture, there is also a very significant fall in the estrogen and progesterone levels. There is also an interesting rise in the relative levels of androgens secreted by the adrenal glands sitting atop the kidneys.

While adjusting to these changes, the woman may go through a feeling of warmth and bodily flushing or the "hot flashes". Most women who are prepared for this ahead of time deal with this in a positive manner. The prospect of not being worried about pregnancy is found by some women to be liberating.

An interesting hormonal effect that can occur around menopause is the relative surge of testosterone from the adrenal cortex. This can lead in some women to a newfound confidence, assertiveness, and resolve that may not have been there before. This may lead the woman to take on the role of the strong and resolute matriarch in many families. There are many examples of women in the postmenopausal years who displayed leadership and strength. Former prime minister of England, Mrs. Margaret Thatcher, also called the "Iron Lady" is a prime example. This is not to simplify her resolution and strength of character that existed before in her life, but to make a point that the postmenopausal rise in androgens may have bolstered her resolve in achieving her goals. It may, in fact, have strengthened her determination in all things. Prime Minister Golda Meir and Prime Minister Indira Gandhi are other examples of women who were considered resolute and strong leaders in their later years.

Other Populations At Higher Risk Of Anxiety:

Homeless Populations:

These individuals are exposed to the vagaries of weather and harassment by the police; they are dependent on other people's goodwill for their support. They often suffer untreated illnesses, malnutrition, and the stress of chronic hunger. At times, they are also victimized by criminals on the street through robbery, assault or sexual exploitation. All of these factors can make for high levels of stress and anxiety in homeless populations.

Veterans:

Soldiers run a high risk of being exposed to life-threatening situations. They are faced with great moral dilemmas of having to take another human being's life or watching other human beings die in front of them and of being unable to offer any help. If they don't get hurt or injured themselves, they may see a significant number of their friends and colleagues get hurt or killed. This can lead to a lifetime of painful memories and sometimes to secondary problems of alcoholism, drug use or PTSD.

Law Enforcement Personnel:

Policemen, during the course of enforcing the law, sometimes have to put their lives at risk and in the line of fire. This is all for the cause of being of service to others, to protect and to serve. They may also not feel fully appreciated by the community for the sacrifices and the risks they undertake. In a time of budget crunches, they have become scapegoats for "waste in the government" when this is the furthest thing from the truth. At times they may be exposed to crime scenes of horrific violence which can be deeply traumatizing. This places policemen and policewomen at higher risk of developing PTSD and other anxiety symptoms. The unpredictability of what they may have to confront on a day-to-day basis may also generate anxiety. Police officers often keep their professional lives private and try to minimize their risks in front of family and friends to avoid worrying them. The family members, however, do understand the risks and may be more prone to anxiety symptoms as consequence of the risks their loved one undertakes.

Workers In Acute Care Psychiatric Units:

The rates of violence in some psychiatric units are quite high. In fact, one of the most dangerous jobs is being a medication nurse in an acute care psychiatric ward. Many psychiatric nurses, psychiatric technicians, psychiatrists, and psychologists become victims of violence from individuals who are in a paranoid or manic state. Being a victim of this violence or witnessing one of your peers become a victim can leave lasting psychological scars.

Firefighters:

Firefighters are regularly exposed to life-threatening situations and scenes of violence. They selflessly go into infernos to rescue others, putting their own lives at risk. This puts them at risk of developing anxiety disorders related to the exposure to traumatic events and the stress of life or death situations. Their risks are similar to the risks taken by military serviceman and law enforcement officers.

Anxiety Risks Unique To Men

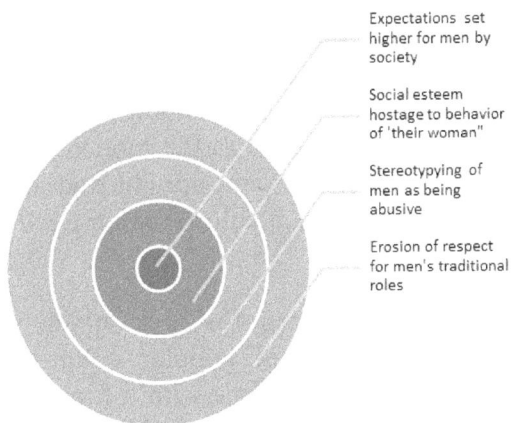

Expectations set higher for men by society

Social esteem hostage to behavior of 'their woman"

Stereotyping of men as being abusive

Erosion of respect for men's traditional roles

Risk Factors for Anxiety in Men

Men also suffer from anxiety for many of same reasons as women do. Men generally are less likely to complain of their anxieties. The general rule for men is to hold your emotions in; the strong, silent type is the preferred male role model in almost every culture.

That silence often covers many anxieties. Men are taught to "never cry" and express emotions or are told that being sentimental is seen to be effeminate and undesirable in men. Men do have a natural tendency to be less expressive but an extreme predilection for suppression of emotions can be unhealthy for them.

Anxieties about not being "manly enough" are common in modern culture. The person in an attempt to be manly may over do the part and avoid being sensitive or kind, believing that this is not the province of "real" men.

The popular culture in the west also stereotypes and promotes this. The typical image of manhood is that of a swashbuckling John Wayne, Clint Eastwood or some other iconic hero who shoots things or blows them up.

A more balanced culture should promote wisdom, patience, kindness, sagacity and courage as the models of manhood. The social activists, scientists and upright statesmen should be given prominence in such cultures among the pantheon of heroes.

In less enlightened cultures, the jock athlete earns the adulation of the media and popular culture and the typical middle aged balding male with a few extra pounds is way down on the totem pole, even if he is the most able, courageous and intelligent man in the house.

Men and their anxieties about being outjocked are similar

to those of women who are comparing themselves to the anorexic waif gracing the magazine covers and held to be a paragon of womanhood.

Men are also mortally afraid that "their woman" will put him down in front of another by overtly or secretly favoring another male. This anxiety is so strong that, if they are confronted by any proof of this being the case, they may go into an acute state of panic. The worst thing that a woman could do would be to fuel this anxiety.

Most women, however, are acutely sensitive of this and are supportive of "their man". They really "stand by their man" and this is to their credit and nothing to be despised. Standing by their man, of course, should not include condoning abusive behaviors by any man towards a woman.

Men should do the same, i.e. "stand by their woman" for the woman can also become insecure. They, too, want to be found acceptable and desirable by the man in their life.

More often nowadays than before, men are having to defend themselves from being labelled chauvinists, sexists or bigots by some sector or other. It is an easy bandwagon to jump on because of the extensive history where men were involved in such acts. It is important, however, not to paint all men with the same broad strokes.

In the modern media, the male is typically represented as a stumbling goofball or a comic character that makes a cameo appearance in the grand theater of life.

The leadership role that men occupied as the one "who wears the pants" is eroding. Although a more equal role for women is a welcome change, this should never come at the cost of denigrating the man or his contributions.

Men are also more likely to be employed in hazardous occupations such as soldiering, firefighter roles and in policing. They therefore run a higher risk of developing stress or PTSD related anxiety due to risks of traumatic exposure in these high risk occupations.

Some cultures promote the use of alcohol by men. Men are judged by their ability to "hold their liquor" and this certainly increases the risk of alcohol dependence and related anxiety problems and complications.

There is a growing men's movement that recognizes the way the changing culture has affected the identity of men. Fathers have less and less time to spend with their sons with divorce being so rampant. Men have a unique and valuable role in culture and they should strive to preserve the best of what it means to be a man.

Anxiety And Intelligence

Most intelligent people tend to be well-adjusted in their lives and are successful at what they do. Some bright people may, however, run a higher risk of suffering from generalized anxiety disorder, obsessive replaying of events and concerns in their mind's eye. Their higher intelligence may sometimes lead to increased risk of slipping on the slopes of logic as they are excessively swayed by the windmills of their mind. They may overly read into situations and, by an exaggerated focus, misinterpret the risk of adverse events. More often than not, however, intelligent people are very prescient, right "on the money", and do well financially and generally outlive everyone else.

From an evolutionary viewpoint, intelligence and a healthy dose of anxiety probably increased the chances of survival.

It was good for a person to be anxious and take precautions when danger lurked in the environment. Such persons were able to take proactive steps to protect themselves from the dangers.

The intelligent people therefore had a greater likelihood of surviving and passing on their genes to their descendants. Because of the survival value of intelligence, every generation has seen the intelligence level of the population increase over time. It seems as if we, as a species, are evolving towards a more sentient, a more self-aware and more well-adapted version of ourselves.

On another note, the intelligent person is a good candidate for psychotherapy. He or she can use that same intelligence to cut through the fog of cognitive distortions.

*Anxiety does not empty tomorrow of its sorrows,
but only empties today of its strength.*

Charles Spurgeon

Chapter 6

An Overview of Treatments

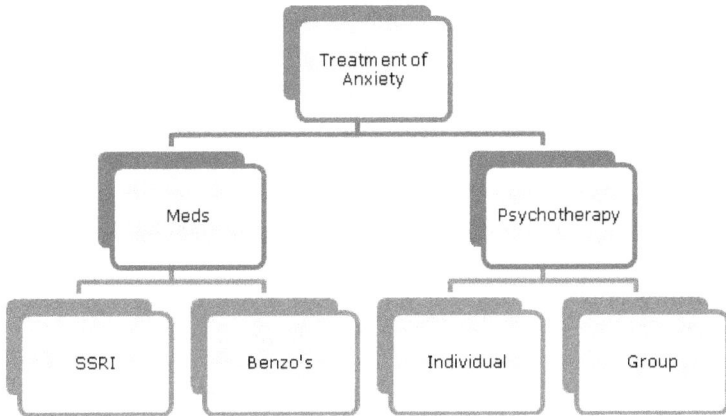

Figure: Some Traditional Approaches

Since the causes of anxiety are diverse, treatment approaches also span the gamut of possible interventions. Thus, treatment for anxiety may be medical or surgical, pharmacological, psychological, social or spiritual in nature. As a general rule, it is good to combine the approaches and target multiple areas of intervention. Some individuals find relief with alternative or complementary treatments such as herbal therapy, acupuncture, acupressure, Ayurvedic procedures, and homeopathic remedies.

The best treatment is always the one that works for you. This may require you to try more than one approach if the first intervention does not work or if it fails to provide full relief of the symptoms.

Social interventions should be attempted to decrease the level of environmental stress whenever possible.

This can be distress related to factors such as unemployment, nutrition and housing issues, abusive relationships, and other areas. The fostering of social supports in those who are isolated and marginalized can be the key to recovery while, at other times, protection from noxious individuals via lodging in shelters for abused individuals can be important. Assistance in obtaining legal help where needed may provide relief for others.

To address any biological components of anxiety, it is usual for the patient to undergo a complete history and physical examination to determine if there are any medical conditions that could be contributing to their anxiety.

If the person is prescribed any medications, these medications should also be thoroughly reviewed to rule out any agents that could be causing anxiety.

If the medical workup reveals a medical cause, then the medical issue is treated. If an offending pharmacological agent is noticed, an alternative agent is substituted that does not cause the side effect of anxiety.

When the medical causes have been ruled out, one must take a careful history about substance and alcohol abuse. This is to rule out the role of alcohol or substance abuse in the causation of anxiety symptoms. When both medical causes and substance abuse causes have been ruled out for the anxiety state, a primary anxiety disorder can be diagnosed.

The patient should be provided support through the initial

workup. The formal treatment plan should be made in collaboration with the patient and other professionals if they are needed and available. A good plan should include interventions in all the spheres, such as medications when indicated, individual therapy, group therapy when indicated, social work assistance for any social issues. If the patient is anxious about medications or traditional treatment, the clinician should put aside his or own preferences and offer the possibility of alternative and complementary treatments available in the community.

Most patients are very grateful for any help received and a simple plan choosing even one or two options initially may suffice in offering relief.

Psychotherapy For Anxiety

Psychotherapy is the art and practice of easing emotional distress in individuals by engaging in a dialogue with them. There are many types of psychotherapy that have been found useful for anxiety and depression

In many therapies, a cognitive model is provided to the patient and this, along with behavioral exercises, is designed to bring about an understanding that the patient can use in his or her day-to-day life.

Some key points to keep in mind about psychotherapy are as follows.

1. Good therapists incorporate aspects of many therapies.

2. Good therapists are eclectic and pick and choose what works for them and their patients.

3. Good therapists work in collaboration with their patients.

There are many types of therapies that are available for the treatment of anxiety. Many of these therapies work by alleviating symptoms of depression as well. The underlying treatment principles in psychotherapy for both conditions are very similar. This implies that a therapy for anxiety will help with depressive symptoms as well.

Some of the common therapies for anxiety and depression are as follows:

Figure: Some Traditional Psychotherapies

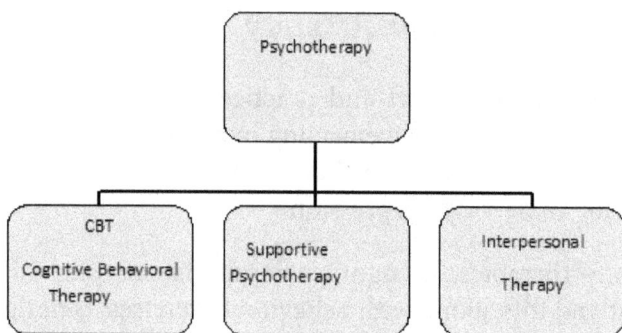

Psychotherapy

CBT
Cognitive Behavioral Therapy

Supportive Psychotherapy

Interpersonal Therapy

Cognitive Behavioral Therapy (CBT)

William James was one of the greatest American thinkers and philosophers. His aphorism that "The greatest weapon against stress is our ability to choose one thought over another" has formed the bedrock of several different psychotherapies including Cognitive Behavioral Therapy, Rational Emotive

Therapy, and Dialectical Behavioral Therapy.

In its essence, CBT focuses on the thoughts behind the anxiety or depression.

The premise of CBT is that irrational thoughts feed almost all negative emotions, such as anxiety, anger, and depression. By correcting the underlying emotional distortion, one can vanquish the dysfunctional emotional state as well.

CBT is based on the idea that cognitions or beliefs that the person carries about the world and about themselves are at the root of all healthy or unhealthy emotions. The therapy posits and asserts that, if the underlying cognitive distortion of a distressful emotion is understood for what it is, its power to cause mischief and misery will be lessened.

The other component of this therapy is to replace the distorted and anxiety-causing belief with its opposite. This is a belief that is undistorted and more conducive to good mental health. This is a belief that leads to a less anxious and less depressed state of mind.

CBT therapy engages the rational side of us and many find it appealing at a common sense level instead of the esoteric psychodynamic formulations about the remote causes of our anxiety or depression.

It has also been tried and tested in the real world with reproducible results when the therapy is carried out with structured manuals designed to aid the psychotherapist.

Clearing Up Cognitive Distortions:
A Diagram

A Computer Virus || **Cognitive Distortions**

Computer with Blue Screen
(Infected with Computer Virus)

⇩

An antivirus software such
as Norton leads to
eradication of erroneous
code of the virus and clears
up the computer screen

Human Being Experiencing
The Blues
(Infested with Cognitive
Distortions)

⇩

Cognitive Behavioral Therapy leads
to removal and replacement of
cognitive Distortions, leading to
Decreased Anxiety, Improved Mood

**Computer Virus Infections and Cognitive Distortions
are similar in some ways**

By identifying feelings and associated thoughts, the
psychotherapist teaches the individual to recognize

distorted thinking. He or she then encourages the patient to replace any distortions with more rational thoughts and conclusions. Through behavioral interventions, practice and encouragement, psychotherapy helps to build the self-confidence of the individual and improve their sense of competency in being able to handle future challenges. The behavioral techniques can also provide exposure to the anxiety-generating stimulus in order to desensitize the individual to that phobia or fear. Psychotherapy has the potential to greatly improve an individual's psychological health and give a person a real chance at freedom from anxiety.

The job of Cognitive Behavioral Therapy is to correct the distortions.

Automatic Wrong Thoughts: We imbibe many ideas about what is expected of us and of what success looks like. The indoctrination starts from very early on in our years by the various advertisements, and cultural prejudices that surround us. When the cultural expectations are distorted, we live with these distortions and do not even realize how these are affecting our happiness and peace of mind. A part of growing up and truly maturing as a human being is the willingness to take a look at every belief we hold and to courageously examine the validity and truth of it.

In some ways we must work out our own salvations. It is not difficult and is within reach. The therapist can act as your guide and cheerleader along the way.

Distortion	Automatic Wrong Thought (AWT)	Corrective Thought (CT)
All or None Thinking	If I don't achieve this goal, I am a total loser.	I can have another go at it. Life is full of second chances. It is not the end of the world.
Catastrophizing/ Magnification of a loss or setback (Making a mountain out of a molehill)	I will never find anyone. I am nothing without him/her. or I will never find another job like that	I can survive without another. It's a big world, someone better is there. Or I will get a better job.
Disqualifying the Positive/ Minimization	The compliments are fake.	I did that job really well. I should be proud of myself.
Emotional Reasoning. -If you feel bad, you expect something to be wrong	I have a bad feeling about this. The project is going to be a disaster.	My mood is bleak because of other things. It will get better
Labeling	I always choke at the crucial moment. I am a loser.	I know what I need to do and can overcome the last minute anxiety. I will be successful.

Distortion	Automatic Wrong Thought (AWT)	Corrective Thought (CT)
Mental Filter.- Looking for the red car- You notice more red cars when you are looking for them.	You see every minor flaw even if it does not matter.	I won't get overworked about minor problems. They can be fixed.
Mind Reading: That others have a negative view of you	S/he probably thinks I am a fool and a loser.	I am not going to rush to conclusions. I don't need everyone's approval
Personalization— attributing yourself as a cause of other's behaviors	He/She didn't even say hello. I must have really botched something.	He/She appeared preoccupied. It does not mean something is wrong or I did something wrong.
Shoulds and Musts. Unreasonable rigid expectations	I should never argue with others.	A healthy debate is good sometimes. It can make the relationship stronger.

Problem Solving Therapy

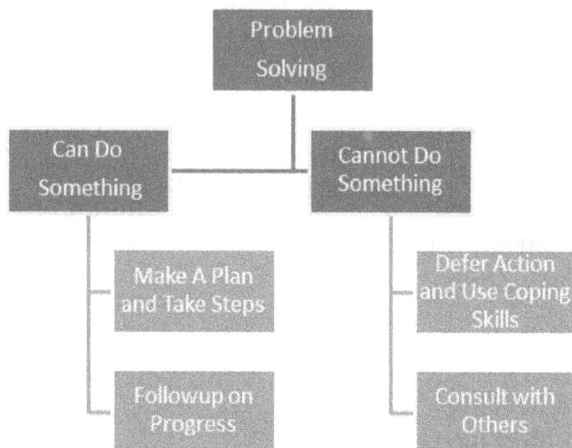

**Approach Every Problem Logically and Make a Rational Plan.
Planning Decreases Anxiety**

Under the stress of anxiety, the ability to rationally think about one's problems may be diminished. Problem solving therapy involves helping the patient solve problems. The therapist can help the patient come to a rational approach to the problem that they are facing. A social worker may be able to help file for needed paperwork and appointments can be made. Help for dependents can be arranged to decrease the level of anxiety around such issues. When a concrete plan is worked out through problem solving therapy, it serves sometimes to lessen anxiety to a far greater degree than would be expected. The therapist must be careful to let the patient take the lead in taking the first steps and offer encouragement and assistance along the way as necessary. It is easy for the person to feel overwhelmed and any social supports that can be recruited or fostered to ally with the patient can also go a long way to ensure the success of the interventions.

Supportive Therapy:

This type of therapy provides emotional support and guidance through a period of crisis in an individual's life. It may be suitable for times when the person is not yet strong enough to be challenged and requires gentle support and a reinforcement of their strengths.

Bibliotherapy:

This therapy involves the use of educational books and literature in order to educate and motivate the patient. Many individuals are able to derive great benefit from reading self-help books or bibliotherapy.

Rational Emotive Therapy: The Common Sense Rational Approach

Your best ally in ridding yourself of anxiety is a rational mind that challenges and rebuts every cognitive distortion and replaces it with a corrective undistorted thought. This therapy is essentially the same as Cognitive Behavioral Therapy. It was promulgated before CBT came into vogue. Once a therapy acquires a catchy acronym such as CBT or DBT, it tends to acquire a following of acolytes who emphasize the minor nuances of each therapy. In the broader perspective however, they are more alike than they are different. They all also share the fact that they do work amazingly well for anxiety, depression and other psychiatric symptoms

Exposure And Desensitization Therapy

Desensitization: This is the gradual exposure of the individual to their feared stimuli. For example, a person afraid of snakes might be allowed at first to visualize a snake. They are asked to imagine their anxiety on a scale from 0-100 with 100 being the worst. At the level of imagining, their anxieties are rated until they gradually decrease, with multiple attempts at imagining to about 50%. The next step will be to actually visualize a snake from 10 feet or more away. This is done through desensitization until they are able to tolerate it and the anxiety level goes down by 50%. Next they are asked to come within 5 feet of a snake that is in a cage. The snake is a non-poisonous one. They are told about the non-poisonous nature and the survivability of the bite.

In this manner, when 50% reduction of the anxiety level is achieved, they can be said to have achieved some level of success. It is important to remember some amount of anxiety to potentially dangerous organisms is desirable and we don't want to eradicate all anxiety for such organisms. We only want to decrease the paralyzing anxiety to a normal level that is found in most people.

This type of desensitization procedure works with almost any anxiety state. It is good to go on a slow gradient and not be too ambitious early on in treatment.

Flooding

The other way to desensitize a person is to flood them with the thing that they fear the most. An example of flooding would be to take that snake and put it around their neck at the very beginning of the therapy.

Treatment of flooding them with too much anxiety may make them feel overwhelmed and fleeing for the nearest exit.

The use of flooding is generally not recommended, but can be effective for some people. Most individuals find the technique to be too stressful and at times it can be counterproductive.

Interpersonal Therapy:

The clinician validates the person and allows for relaxed interactions. Feedback about interaction may be provided to help the patient become more aware of their patterns of interaction and the reasons for these. The therapist and the patient may explore if this pattern has a linkage to more historical relationships from the past.

The person eventually gains control over dysfunctional interactions and anxiety associated with these.

Supportive Therapy:

This is to provide the patient unconditional positive regard and help shore up their defenses.

The mainstays of therapy are to avoid confrontation and to provide encouragement for positive gains.

PROGRESSIVE MUSCLE RELAXATION

This therapy involves teaching the patient relaxation skills such as deep breathing exercises and progressive muscle relaxation when faced with anxiety. The individual is taught to control hyperventilation and to control the muscle tension that accompanies anxiety states.

Psychodynamic Therapy

Sometimes there may be secondary conscious or unconscious gains derived from keeping the dysfunctional emotions. This may include having an excuse for failure, e.g. "I cannot succeed because I have had terrible relationships," or "She took it all out of me," or other such refrains. There may be underlying fear of failure. Sometimes there is a fear of success in some individuals that don't do well on exams. It is like the fear of the alcoholic who is afraid to get better lest he or she disappoint the spouse that has come to expect failure from the alcoholic. The root is often in a dysfunctional relationship that needs to be examined and brought out into the light of day through psychotherapy or courageous introspection.

When another's identity is tied to seeing you denigrated or rescuing you from your failure, it is a sad situation for that person but damnation for you.

Decide to succeed and let the others be disappointed if they will be by your success.

If the underlying psychodynamic issues are not laid bare and exposed to the cleansing light of awareness, these dark forces may continue to cause dysfunction in different ways. You can get this monkey off your back for the rest of your life with the help of a good psychotherapist and sometimes with your own efforts and diligence.

Catharsis:

One of the therapeutic approaches is to revisit traumatic memories of the past and process them by going over the details in as vivid a form as possible. Sometimes more than one accounting is necessary. After the memory has been processed, it is helpful to look for anything similar in the past and process that as well until the memories no longer stir emotion or conflict in your mind. Once the experience has been exorcised or processed in such a way with the help of a supportive and empathic therapist, it can lead to a lifting of that emotional burden. This can be a very liberating experience for the individual. The time to achieve relief via this therapy will vary in individuals.

Combining Psychotherapy And Medications Can Be A Good Thing

It is the prevailing wisdom that pharmacotherapy should always be combined with psychotherapy. Psychotherapy however can be effective by itself for mild to moderate cases and may require only minimal or no pharmacological intervention.

When prescribing medications to a patient for anxiety, psychotherapy is also offered to teach the patient about their condition and the psychological factors that may be contributing to their anxiety symptoms. Psychotherapy can teach the patient to recognize their dysfunctional thought patterns. They are then encouraged to replace the distorted thoughts with the correct conclusions.

Sometimes the causes of anxiety are more deep-seated than mere distortions of cognition. For these occasions, psychodynamic and interpersonal therapy can reveal the hidden motives and repressed memories that may be at the root of their anxieties.

Social interventions, including assistance with housing, and guidance in regards to other financial, legal, or housing difficulties can be of immense help in mitigating anxiety.

There may also be complex issues related to dysfunctional social relationships. There may be other social issues that are stoking the fire of anxiety, such as the person feeling trapped in a crime-ridden neighborhood or being chronically unemployed or underemployed.

By being aware and cognizant of the social difficulties of the patient and by trying to help where possible, the clinician can offer empathy, guidance, and support as needed.

Some of the ways that we can make social interventions include hands-on help with the filing of forms for disability, rent assistance, jobs, etc. It may also include referrals for support groups, fostering of social support networks, and problem solving for other real life problems.

Exercise And Walking As Therapy For Anxiety And Depression

Walking is the consummate exercise. It exercises almost all the muscles in the body in a manner that is natural as possible. It also provides an opportunity for one to be outside in fresh air and also exposes the skin to sunlight which can help in generating adequate amounts of vitamin D. The role of vitamin D in the human body is complex and most individuals in technologically advanced societies are deficient in this vitamin. This is because they spend an unnatural amount of time indoors sheltered from the rays of the sun. This prevents the chemical reaction between sunlight and the human skin that is needed for the formation of vitamin D.

Being outdoors may also connect you with nature in other ways that are meaningful and therapeutic.

Our first steps as a human being at around one year of age were thrilling and joyful; we couldn't believe the freedom that our walking brought us.

If you decide to take up walking, make sure to invest in some good walking shoes. They can make a difference to how tired your feet feel.

Make sure that you are healthy enough for the level of exercise that you plan to undertake.

Walk at your own pace and gradually increase the amount. Pedometers are available that you can strap to your waist belt. It is been recommended that a person should take about 10,000 steps per day. This works out to about 5 miles. It is calculated on the premise that the average stride is about two and half feet. 2,000 steps becomes about 5,000 feet or a mile. 10,000 steps become about 5 miles. This is equal to about 8 kilometers. The distance may vary slightly for different stride lengths but this is about the average.

The average sedentary person takes about 1,000 steps per day. By gradually increasing the number of steps taken per day, one can reach the goal of 10,000 steps per day in a month without undue physical stress.

The increase in the number of steps should not exceed 500 steps a day.

Some activities that can help increase walking are as follows:

Taking the dog for a walk

Walking with a friend, child, or spouse, or having a walking meeting with a co-worker

Parking further from the office or store entrance

Walking to nearby stores whenever possible

Walking around the house whenever possible

Walking in the neighborhood

It is therapeutic to participate in any sport activity due to the social interaction, camaraderie that it fosters and the physical exercise that it provides.

Other neurochemical events that occur with exercise may normalize us and bring us back to our natural state. Our natural state could be defined as when we struggled to gather food by walking, jumping, climbing, and whatever was needed in our role as a hunter-gatherer species long ago.

If you have much physical exertion during the day, sleep will come to you naturally and blissfully without the need of any medications. This is the common observation of many people, but no neurochemical correlation has ever been sought as to how exercise helps with sleep.

The fact that we don't know the details of how exercise alters neurochemistry should not detract or deter us from utilizing this useful and beneficial effect. As mentioned elsewhere, exercise truly is the most underutilized medicine.

This means that a return to nature may yield benefits whose neurochemical cause and explanation may lie beyond our wits at this time. That does not mean that it does not exist. We must therefore strive to return to a natural state of being in order reach our optimum health and functioning. Our natural state is to be hopeful and joyous. We are by nature inclined to contentment, mirth, and laughter and the absence of this for long is certainly unnatural. By following healthy habits, we can recover from our anxiety state. By being our natural selves, and leading a healthy lifestyle that incorporates adequate amounts of exercise and exposure to the outdoor natural environment, we can achieve our natural state of joy and contentment—and also prevent the return of anxiety and misery.

Some Points to Keep In Mind:

The main risks of walking outdoors are exposure to allergens and risks for violence in a violent neighborhood.

If you are allergic to bees, carry your Epi kit on you and avoid wearing perfume which may attract honeybees. An Epi kit is an emergency kit given to individuals who have severe allergies. It consists of a syringe preloaded with epinephrine that automatically injects the life-saving medication after the person jabs the point of the needle in the lateral aspect of the thigh. It is used if and when stung by a bee or exposure to the allergen (the substance the person is allergic to).

You should have someone preferably come with you on the walk if this is a hazard. You can also do the walking indoors on a treadmill, an indoor track, or walk in place if all else is unavailable.

If there is a risk of environmental violence, unnecessary exposure to risk should be avoided. If you do go out, have a companion with you or take other precautions as needed.

Progressive Muscle Relaxation

This exercise involves progressively tensing alternating muscle groups and releasing them. One starts at the feet and follows a script that instructs the person to move from one group of muscles to the next, tensing and releasing each group until the cycle of tensing and releasing has progressed from the feet to the head. The results are remarkably good for such a simple exercise.

The progressive muscle relaxation script is given below. You can record it on your smartphone and play it back whenever you want to relax. Remember to pause for 15 or more seconds between directions for each muscle group in order for the relaxation from the recently contracted muscle group to be experienced.

PMR Instructions:

Find a quiet place where you will not be disturbed for 10 to 15 minutes.

Take a long, slow and deep breath.

Gradually curl your toes downward and feel the tension in the soles of your feet.

Hold your breath for a few seconds and then release, and along with it, release the tension in your feet.

Now move your attention to your lower legs and curl your toes upwards towards your knees and feel the tension at the back of your calves.

Take a deep breath and hold it for just a few seconds, then let it out and let the tension in your legs also be released.

Now move your attention to your thighs and try to raise your legs if lying down, or try to drive down your heels if you're sitting down, and feel the tension in your legs.

Take a deep breath and hold it for a few seconds before releasing it along with the release of tension in your leg.

Take a 15-second pause and feel the relaxation spread.

Next, tighten the muscles in your hip and buttock area. Hold this for a few seconds and then release your breath and let the muscles relax.

Now, bring your attention to your stomach and contract your stomach muscles as if you are trying to touch your belly button to your spine.

Hold your breath for a few seconds then release it and release the muscle tension in your stomach area.

Next, bring your attention to the muscles in your back. Tense them in the same way and relax them after a few seconds by taking in a deep breath, tensing, and then releasing the breath and releasing the tension.

Next, tense your shoulders in the same way by taking in a deep breath, hold it and let go of your breath and let go of the tension.

Do the same procedure with the muscles in your chest and in your neck areas.

Try to pull the shoulders up to your neck area, tense them while breathing in and let them relax with the exhalation.

Repeat this same procedure with the upper arms lower arms and the hands.

Tighten the muscles in your face by squeezing your eyes and lips closed and then let them relax.

Next, open your jaw as wide as you can for a few seconds and then relax.

You should now be relaxed from your toes to your face.

Take in a few deep slow breaths and enjoy the relaxed feeling.

It is an easily learned and very simple exercise that helps to ease muscle tension. It has the effect of decreasing psychological tension and anxiety as well.

Biofeedback And Anxiety

Biofeedback is the simple process of providing visual feedback to a person about their physiological state via electrodes hooked up from their skin or scalp to a monitor they can view. A therapist trains the person in a relaxation technique such as progressive muscle relaxation or mindfulness meditation and allows them to see the type of brain wave pattern and the heart rate and skin conductance associated with a relaxed state. In due time, they can train themselves to voluntarily produce the physiological response such as a brain wave pattern associated with relaxation. The technique works and is usually available at bigger centers such as teaching hospitals and specialized clinics.

This availability seems to be its only drawback at this point. It needs to be emphasized that the patient is taught effective relaxation techniques such as meditation, muscle relaxation, or others. The biofeedback process teaches them that they can control their anxiety symptoms. By doing this multiple times, it gives them the confidence that they can do this at will. This granting of a sense of mastery to the individual is a significant component of the overall therapeutic benefit of biofeedback treatment for anxiety.

Some companies such as "Life Matters" sell home devices for feedback that may be helpful for anxiety symptoms. Their web address is http://www.lifematters.com/about_us.asp

Promoting The Natural Healing Of The Mind

This is a hypothesis, but I believe that the brain attempts to heal itself from any malady it suffers much like any other organ that is under stress. Just as the liver, a broken bone or a tear in the skin tries to heal itself, the brain, I believe, also has natural mechanisms that it activates to deal with excessive anxiety or depression.

The key to recovery may be to facilitate these natural efforts of the brain. In the same way that we tell a patient not to peel the scabs over their healing skin wounds, we should avoid re-stressing the individual who is trying heal from a traumatic event. We should just provide a calming environment and a supportive presence. If we allow a person time to heal in a peaceful environment, allow his body to keep the normal routines of sleep and some amount of physical work, a natural healing should take place.

To this end, vacations are useful in that they provide relief from stressors that may pervade the environment and allow a silent space for the individual to heal. In a matter of a few weeks, the person may find their moods lifting. Sometimes a brief vacation for 2 to 3 days that allows the person to cocoon in their comfort zone can be very healing.

Religious sanctuaries such as churches, gurudwaras and temples or mosques may also provide relief. Allowing and encouraging the person to have routines for meditation also provide these quiet spaces. It is these quiet spaces and quiet times that protect us from excessive stress and allow us to heal in a natural and wholesome way.

As an example of the brain trying to heal itself, one can note that early morning awakening is prompted by the brain of the person who is severely depressed. Studies have shown that early morning awakening promotes a lifting of the mood as does some amount of sleep deprivation. Is this the brain trying to heal itself by some unknown neurochemical mechanism that triggers early morning awakening?

Perhaps one approach to healing may be advice for the patient to get up early in the morning, and be exposed to the first rays of the sun which have a different spectrum and may have added therapeutic benefits for the individual. Perhaps the key to healing is to bring life back to as normal a state as possible where people wake with the morning chirping of the birds and retire when the darkness of the night falls.

Claude Bernard, the brilliant French physiologist, coined the phrase *milieu interior*. The concept is that the human body has evolved to exist in a state of an enduring stable milieu that we have now incorporated within ourselves. This embodiment of the primordial constant milieu includes our constant set body temperature, the constant alkalinity or pH of our blood, and an optimum state of hydration. The main job of almost all the organs of the body is to maintain this constant environment on the inside that is optimum for us. The constant milieu interior also includes an optimum neurochemistry of the brain and, when it is affected, the brain can be expected to enact certain mechanisms to bring the neurochemical state to its optimum milieu interior state.

The natural state of human beings is to be happy, kind, sociable, and hopeful. The natural state of human beings is to smile easily, to be able to trust others and to be able to adapt to some amount of limited change. The natural state is to be social with others and find our place in our own community. When the natural state is disturbed, it sets into motion a series of adaptive changes which attempt to recreate the natural alignment. When these attempts fail, stress is generated and pathology may arise in the body or mind.

Psychotherapy may provide a sense of coherence that is lost at such times of stress. The great task of psychotherapy is to guide the person towards re-establishing a natural state of relationship with his or her environment.

Making a successful external adjustment to the social milieu may result in secondary changes in the neurochemistry that allows for remission of the psychological symptoms.

Psychotherapy assists the person in adapting to change. Medications are like splints for a broken bone that create the environment that allows for healing to occur faster than it ordinarily would. Psychotherapy is like mopping up a slippery floor so that the person does not slip and fracture the bone again.

All other therapeutic events are those that decrease conflict and stress in the environment. They are all attempts at making the floor less slippery for the individual. The mental disorder is the broken bone.

As a general rule, a multilevel approach is the best approach when it comes to the treatment of psychiatric disorders. This means that medications alone will not solve the whole problem of anxiety without a thoughtful plan for education, social interventions, and psychotherapy as needed for support of the individual.

Pharmacological Treatment Of Anxiety.

Pharmacological agents from several different classes are used to provide relief from anxiety. Many of the medications were put through double-blind placebo-controlled trials before FDA approval was granted to them.

The exact mechanism of action of the medications that are used for anxiety is not fully understood but we do know that one of their actions is to cause an increase in the levels of one or more of the following neurotransmitters within the junctions (synapses) between brain cells. These neurotransmitters are serotonin, norepinephrine, dopamine, and gamma amino butyric acid (GABA)

The great mystery of how these changes finally translate into a lifting of the anxiety and depressive symptoms is a challenge that remains for future neuroscientists to resolve.

Some Common Antidepressants

GENERIC NAME	BRAND NAME	THERAPEUTIC DOSE RANGE	INDICATIONS/ NOTES
FLUOXETINE	PROZAC	20 TO 80 MGS	ANTIDEPRESSANT, PANIC DISORDER, OCD,
PAROXETINE	PAXIL, PAXIL CR	20 TO 50 MGS	SOCIAL ANXIETY, GENERALIZED ANXIETY, MAY INTERACT WITH TOHER MEDS, PREGNANCY PRECAUTIONS
SERTRALINE	ZOLOFT	25 TO 200 MGS	FOR PTSD, OCD, GENERALIZED ANXIETY, LESS INTERACTIONS WITH OTHER MEDS
CITALOPRAM	CELEXA	10 TO 40 MGS	ANTIDEPRESSANT, ANTIANXIETY EFFECTS, GET EKG AT 40 MGS
ESCITALOPRAM	LEXAPRO	5 TO 20 MGS	SAME AS ABOVE, CHECK EKG AT 20 MGS OR ABOVE
MIRTAZEPINE	REMERON	15 TO 45 MGS	FOR DEPRESSION, ANXIETY, INSOMNIA, POOR APPETITE
VENLAFAXINE	EFFEXOR, EFFEXOR XR	37.5 TO 225 MGS	DUAL MECHANISM, EFFECTIVE FOR DEPRESSION, ANXIETY, CHECK FOR ELEVATED BLOOD PRESSURE AT HIGHER DOSAGE

GENERIC NAME	BRAND NAME	THERAPEUTIC DOSE RANGE	INDICATIONS/ NOTES
IMIPRAMINE	TOFRANIL	25 TO 200 MGS	TRICYCLIC ANTIDEPRESSANT, EFFECTIVE FOR DEPRESSION, PANIC DISORDER
CLOMIPRAMINE	ANAFRANIL	25 TO 250 MGS	MOSTLY SEROTONERGIC, GOOD FOR OCD
FLUVOXAMINE	LUVOX	50 TO 300 MGS	FOR OCD

The human brain is an amazingly complex achievement of evolution and we are at best working with empirical results and logical conjectures. It is much like the way physicians used the plant foxglove for treating heart failure in the 19th century with effectiveness without knowing about the active ingredients in the plant. It was only much later that digoxin was discovered to be the active ingredient and its selective inhibition of the plasma membrane sodium pump was found to be the underlying therapeutic mechanism.

And so while we do not know the entire cascade of neurological events, we do know that medication brings relief for individuals who suffer from anxiety or depression. They have proven themselves to be more beneficial than placebos in multiple objective studies.

The following classes of medication are used for treating anxiety.

SSRIs (Serotonin Reuptake Inhibitors)
SNRIs
Benzodiazepines
Buspirone
Tricyclic Antidepressants
MAOIs

When deciding on the choice of medication for treating an anxiety disorder, individual practitioners have different preferences. One person may have a preference for SSRI (Serotonin Reuptake Inhibitors) to be the first line treatment option for anxiety. The other school of thought gives preference for the use of benzodiazepines as the first line treatment.

Both schools of thought have some valid reasons for their choices. The points in favor of the SSRIs include the fact that they also treat any co-occurring depression. The other advantage for this choice is that SSRI's or SNRI's are not abuse risk medications.

The benzodiazepine group argues that the benzodiazepines are safe medication for a majority of the population in terms of addiction risk, have a quicker onset of benefit, and are relatively nontoxic. They work quickly and are free of noxious side effects other than initial sedation or the occasional disinhibition in some patients.

It is prudent for the wise physician to keep an open mind about both treatment options and use whatever works best for the individual patient.

A Brief History Of SSRI's (Selective Serotonin Reuptake Inhibitors) :

The first SSRI fluoxetine was manufactured in 1972 and was later marketed as Prozac in 1987 when it was approved by the FDA for the treatment of depression. It became a blockbuster drug for the drug company Lily.

It was remarkably effective for the treatment of depression and had none of the worrisome side effects of the tricyclics. It was also not lethal in overdose which was a constant catch-22 for the prescribing physician prior to the advent of SSRIs. The prescription of tricyclic antidepressants had to be limited in amount to avoid a lethal overdose. Even with the best monitoring, there was the risk that the patient would hoard these medications and attempt suicide by overdose later. The period when the patient was just coming out of depression was especially risky for some patients.

The advent of this novel agent led to reports of unexpected benefits for some patients. Reports began to emerge that Prozac was changing long-standing neurotic traits in some individuals. These had previously been found to be beyond the pale of psychopharmacology and patients were consigned to years of psychotherapy that yielded meagre benefits at best.

The changes to neurotic personality traits in some cases were so remarkable that it made the news. Dr. Peter Kramer wrote a book on the subject titled *Listening to Prozac* that was acclaimed for its insightful observations and conclusions.

Long-held convoluted theories about the causes of "neurotic anxiety" were called into question when a simple chemical began to help these individuals come out of their crusty and rigid shells.

In the late 80's, it seemed to some that the brave new world for better or worse was truly at hand where there would be a fix for everything that ailed mankind. Such visions, of course, were grandiose and uninformed by the complexities of real life.

In 1991, sertraline (Zoloft) was launched, followed in 1993 by paroxetine (Paxil). Citalopram (Celexa) came to the market in 1998 and in 2000 Lexapro was introduced. Fluvoxamine (Luvox) has been present since 1993. It, however, has been utilized mostly for OCD and is rarely used for anxiety or depression.

The Different SSRI's:

The different SSRIs include fluoxetine (Prozac), paroxetine (Paxil), sertraline (Zoloft), citalopram (Celexa), Ecitalopram (Lexapro), and fluvoxamine (Luvox). A tricyclic antidepressant clomipramine (Anafranil) is also predominantly a SSRI agent and is sometimes chosen specifically as a first-line treatment for obsessive-compulsive disorder (OCD).

General Guidelines for Prescribers:

Citalopram (Celexa), escitalopram (Lexapro) and sertraline (Zoloft) are preferred by clinicians when the patient is on several other medications because they do not have many interactions with other medications. If using other SSRIs, and especially with fluvoxamine (Luvox), it is important to check for any drug interactions with other prescribed drugs as there can be a serious rise in levels of other medications due to the enzyme inhibiting properties of fluvoxamine (Luvox), fluoxetine (Prozac) and Paroxetine (Paxil).

It is customary to start any medication at a lower than normal dosage for anxiety-disordered patients as they seem to be acutely sensitive to side effects. The dose is then taken up to the standard treatment dose for that agent in a gradual manner. The dose is held at this level for a period of four weeks and an assessment of the state of anxiety is then made.

This is usually done by feedback from the patient to the doctor and sometimes by various rating scales such as the Hamilton anxiety rating scale. Both the methods work equally well.

If there is no benefit in 4 weeks, the dose of the SSRI is raised and a period of another 2 to 4 weeks is allowed to gauge the response. Cognitive Behavioral Therapy (CBT) or other chosen type of individual therapy is continued while the medication is being adjusted for optimal dosage. If there is no benefit at 6 to 8 weeks, a trial of an alternative SSRI is recommended although many clinicians would prefer to go to an agent that has a dual mechanism of action (both a serotonin-enhancing as well as a norepinephrine a-enhancing effect). These dual agents are called SNRIs (Serotonin Norepinephrine reuptake inhibitors).

SSRI withdrawal syndrome:

The SSRI paroxetine (Paxil) and fluvoxamine (Luvox) have a shorter half-life than other SSRIs. Due to this, patients may experience a withdrawal syndrome when these medications are discontinued. A similar withdrawal syndrome with venlafaxine has also been mentioned. The withdrawal syndrome is mild and can be marked by depression, dizziness, stomach distress, fatigue and muscle pains. It can be prevented by a slow taper or by cross covering with a longer acting agent such as fluoxetine (Prozac).

SSRI risks and benefits:

Paxil is not recommended in pregnant women or those who could become pregnant. There are a few limited reports of cardiac-anomalies in children born to mothers that are on Paxil.

For sertraline (Zoloft) absorption can be improved if given with food. The presence or absence of food does not appear to be a factor in the absorption of the other SSRIs.

Citalopram [Celexa]: The dosage is limited to 40 mg as there may be some risk of cardiac conduction delay at higher doses. An EKG is recommended if citalopram (Celexa) or escitalopram (Lexapro) is used at the higher doses.

Side effects of SSRIs:

SSRIs are generally safe and well tolerated as far as medications go.

There are some reports of decreased libido in about 17% of individuals who are on long-term maintenance SSRI medications. Most individuals do not notice this or report this to be an issue. The libido is improved generally from the time of depression when the SSRI was originally started. Although generally perceived as being weight neutral, they may add a few pounds in some individuals.

Some patients may be acutely sensitive to the sedating effects of mirtazapine (Remeron). SSRIs should be prescribed with caution in those with bleeding tendencies as the inhibition of serotonin reuptake may impair platelet aggregation and increase bleeding risk during surgery in some cases.

Starting an SSRI

The patient is offered a trial of an SSRI at half the normal starting dose if anxiety symptoms are significant. After a period of one week the dosage is raised to a current recommended dose of fluoxetine (Prozac) 20 mg a day. The patient is allowed to stay on this dose for a period of 3-4 weeks to monitor for a response. If there is no significant response by four weeks, the dosage can be raised, and the patient can be monitored for the next 2 to 3 weeks. If there's no response to the SSRI, it is recommended that a different SSRI be tried. If this is also ineffective, an SNRI such as Effexor or Remeron may be used. Remeron is quite sedating and activates the appetite and hence may be an ideal agent when there is decreased sleep and appetite. The risk of increased appetite, of course, is obesity and all the problems that come with obesity. Mirtazapine (Remeron) also acts as an effective antianxiety agent for some individuals.

Another 4 to 8 weeks should be allowed with therapeutic dosage to monitor a response.

In the beginning, a low dose of benzodiazepine—such as lorazepam (Ativan) 0.5 mg in the morning and evening or clonazepam (Klonopin) 0.5 mg once or twice a day—may be offered until the other agents kick in and start providing their antianxiety and antidepressant benefits.

As with all psychiatric medications, an informed consent is necessary. The zealous healer in the clinician wants to make the patient get better as soon as possible. The decision to take the medication however is ultimately the prerogative of the patient and they must be allowed to make the decision even if it is contrary to the recommendation of the doctor.

The only exception is when the illness causes a risk to the life of the individual or a threat to the safety of others. In such cases, any physician is allowed to administer emergency medications and a legal process exists in every jurisdiction for obtaining court orders for involuntary medications for the health and safety of the patient impaired by mental illness. Involuntary medications for anxiety disorder are rarely indicated but maybe a possibility if there is a severe comorbid depression that endangers the individual.

SNRI's (Serotonin Norepinephrine Reuptake Inhibitors):

The following medications represent this class: venlafaxine (Effexor), desvenlafaxine (Pristiq), and duloxetine (Cymbalta), the most popular of these agents is venlafaxine

(Effexor XR (Extended Release) or Effexor (Regular Release). The extended release is preferred because the regular release venlafaxine has a notable side effect in some people of causing nausea and dyspepsia.

If the regular release venlafaxine is used (because it is more affordable), the initial gastrointestinal side effects of nausea can be lessened by giving the dose of the medication with food and starting at a lower dosage of 37.5 mgs and gradually building up the dose. The nausea is related in part to the initial rise in blood levels and the food slows down the absorption to provide a smoother rise of levels. The starting dose is usually 37.5 mg for Effexor and this is titrated up to 75 mg after four days and then after another 4 to 5 days is titrated up to the therapeutic dose of 150 mgs. The extended release version is also started at the same dosage ranges and titrated over the same time period.

It is sensible to be slow with the titration as there are no immediate benefits from the antidepressant anyhow and there is no point in causing side effects early on due to too rapid a titration. This can turn the patient away from a useful and potentially life-enhancing medication.

For the record, most individuals are able to tolerate a more rapid titration of Effexor XR 75mgs for 3 to 4 days and then a raising of the dose to 150 mgs without ill effects. This may be needed if the patient is admitted to an inpatient unit where time for titration may be limited.

During the follow-up visits for patients on venlafaxine, it is useful to periodically check the blood pressure and vitals as venlafaxine may cause a mild rise of blood pressure at the higher doses. The maximum dose is 225 mgs and the usual therapeutic dose is 150 mgs for most individuals.

The patient is treated at this dose for 4 to 6 weeks and the anxiety is measured by clinical assessment and sometimes also by objective rating scales. If there is no therapeutic response in 4 to 6 weeks, the medication may be augmented with buspirone or a benzodiazepine.

The SSRI agents Prozac, Zoloft, Paxil, citalopram or Celexa, and Lexapro have all been used with benefit for generalized anxiety disorder, panic disorder, social anxiety disorder and obsessive-compulsive disorder (OCD). They all work.

It all comes down to which medication causes the fewest side effects with the person and interacts the least with the other medications that they may be on.

The SSRI agent paroxetine (Paxil) was the first SSRI approved by the FDA for social anxiety disorder. Although other SSRI agents may also be effective this agent has been found to be particularly effective by many clinicians who have prescribed it for social anxiety problems. Pregnant women should avoid this and if the patient is on other medications, a drug interaction check should be run to avoid such problems in view of its enzyme inhibiting effects.

The SSRI sertraline (Zoloft) was first approved by the FDA for PTSD. It is an effective agent for this condition but other SSRIs have also shown themselves to be beneficial for treating PTSD. As mentioned earlier, it should be given with food and started at a low dose. Infrequently, it can cause gastrointestinal complaints of nausea and diarrhea in some patients. If this occurs, the agent should be switched for a different SRRI. Some clinicians tend to persevere at lower dosages and the sideeffects do abate for some of the patients with time. Most clinicians find it simpler to make the switch instead.

The agent fluvoxamine (Luvox) is beneficial for the treatment of OCD and other anxiety states but can have some serious interactions with the metabolism of other medications due to its enzyme-inhibiting properties. If it is prescribed, there needs to be a careful check for any drug interactions.

SSRI meds are effective first line meds for generalized anxiety disorder and other anxiety states.

SSRIs should be strictly avoided with MAOIs as this can result in a lethal and dangerous syndrome of serotonin toxicity called the serotonin syndrome. There should ideally be a window of 6 to 8 weeks after the discontinuation of a MAOI inhibitor. There should also be a window of 6 to 8 weeks after discontinuation of the longer acting SSRIs, such as fluoxetine, which have active metabolites with very long half-lives.

Benzodiazepines:

These are important and generally safe medications for the treatment of anxiety. The benefits are often evident the same day that the medications are started. There is no waiting period of 3 to 4 weeks before obtaining relief.

There has been a great deal of hoopla about the drug abuse and drug dependence liability of these agents. Studies have actually shown that most people do not become addicted to benzodiazepines. They use them in a therapeutic manner.

An exception to this rule exists if there is a history of substance or alcohol abuse. In such cases, there is a risk that the person may try to abuse benzodiazepines.

Due care and caution therefore needs to be exercised in such circumstances. One clue as to whether the person is abusing these substances and prescription medications is to find out if they are becoming more dysfunctional on them.

If dysfunction is evident, such as being over sedated or disinhibited, these meds should be discontinued.

Most patients do well on a low dose of a benzodiazepine and prescriber should not feel overly intimidated by the prospect of abuse or diversion if the patient does not have such a history in the past.

Sideeffects of Benzodiazepines:

One of the salient side effects is sedation. If the individual is sedated or sleepy due to the medication, the dose should be lowered and they should be cautioned to avoid driving or operating any dangerous machinery.

Over time, tolerance develops to the sedating effect but does not develop to the anxiolytic (anxiety-dissolving) effect. Patients therefore are able to obtain benefit for anxiety without being sedated.

The benzodiazepines commonly used include the following: lorazepam (Ativan), alprazolam (Xanax), diazepam (Valium), temazepam (Restoril), oxazepam (Serax), and chlordiazepoxide (Librium).

Withdrawal symptoms may occur if the steady intake of short-acting benzodiazepines is interrupted. The withdrawal anxiety may be superimposed on any baseline anxiety and thus complicate assessment of the original anxiety and any response to the treatment.

Short anxiety agents such as alprazolam (Xanax) earned much notoriety in the 90's due to withdrawal seizures that occurred in some individuals who were abusing this benzodiazepine. It generally takes about 2 to 3 weeks of regular around the clock use of a sedating agent to induce dependence and withdrawal.

Longer acting benzodiazepines such as clonazepam (Klonopin) do not have the acute withdrawal anxiety that the shorter acting agents such as lorazepam (Ativan) or alprazolam (Xanax) usually have. Xanax has been formulated into a long-acting preparation which overcomes the anxiety that the shorter acting agent had of midday withdrawal anxiety.

The two benzodiazepines that are at a higher risk for being abused are diazepam (Valium) and alprazolam (Xanax). They should be avoided, in high risk patients.

The Benzodiazepines

GENERIC NAME	BRAND NAME	EQUIVALENT DOSE	HALF LIFE	INDICATIONS/ NOTES
ALPRAZOLAM	XANAX	0.5 MG	6 TO 9 HRS	ANTI-ANXIETY HIGHER ABUSE RISK
LORAZEPAM	ATIVAN	1 MG	10-20 HRS	ANTI-ANXIETY, AVAILABLE FOR INTRAMUSCULAR USE
CLONAZEPAM	KLONOPIN	0.5 MG	18 – 50 HRS	ANTI-ANXIETY, ANTICONVULSANT, ADJUNCTIVE MOOD STABILIZER
DIAZEPAM	VALIUM	5 MG	20- 100 HRS	ANTI ANXIETY, MUSCLE RELXANT, SOMEWHAT HIGHER RISK FOR ABUSE
ESTAZOLAM	PROSOM	1 MG	10-20 HRS	HYPNOTIC, ANTIANXIETY

GENERIC NAME	BRAND NAME	EQUIVALENT DOSE	HALF LIFE	INDICATIONS/ NOTES
TEMAZEPAM	RESTORIL	20 MGS	8 -22 HRS	HYPNOTIC, ANTIANXIETY
CHLORDIAZEPOXIDE	LIBRIUM	25 MGS	30-100 HRS	ANTIANXIETY, OFTEN USED FOR DETOX FROM ALCOHOL

Buspirone (Buspar):

This is a non-benzodiazepine antianxiety agent that is used when there is a concern about the abuse liability of benzodiazepines. This can occur if the patient has a history of alcohol or substance abuse. The usual starting dose is 10 to 15 mg twice a day. It is titrated up to 40 mg if there is no response in 2 to 3 weeks. The dose may be raised up to 60 mg if relief remains insufficient. Some clinicians recommend raising the dose to 45 mg initially in order to increase the chances of an initial response. The time to onset of benefits is 2 to 4 weeks but sometimes a longer period is needed. When used in conjunction with psychotherapy such as CBT, it can be quite effective. It is well tolerated and tends to have few interactions with other medications except for the MAOI agents.

Pregabablin: This medication is similar in structure to a natural compound in the brain called gamma amino butyric acid (GABA). It is currently approved by the FDA for the management of neuropathic pain and post-herpetic neuralgia. It is also used at times as adjunctive therapy in patients with partial onset seizures. It has shown some benefit for generalized anxiety disorder and the benefits are apparent in about a week. It is an anticonvulsant and gradual tapering off is recommended if the medication is to be discontinued for any reason after starting it.

Gabapentin: This agent also acts on the GABA receptors and is reported in clinical case studies to be effective for anxiety symptoms for some patients.

Hydroxyzine (Vistaril): The antihistamine hydroxyzine has also been found to be useful in the treatment of anxiety states. It is mildly sedating, and has some anticholinergic sideeffects which may result in constipation or urinary hesitance in some individuals at the higher dosages.

Antipsychotic Agents: These are generally not recommended for anxiety. They have been used in the most severe cases of anxiety states such as OCD (Obsessive Compulsive Disorder) or PTSD (Post Traumatic Stress Disorder) by some clinicians with some benefit. Some of these medications include agents such as ziprasidone (Geodon), quetiapine (Seroquel). These agents are less likely to cause weight gain and therefore may be preferred over other antipsychotic agents.

Tricyclic Antidepressants:

Although these medications are marketed as antidepressants, they are quite effective for certain anxiety disorders such as Panic Disorder.

They are also excellent agents for the treatment of serious depression. Except for clomipramine (Anafranil), all of the tricyclics primarily act by inhibiting the norepinephrine reuptake and thereby increasing the level of norepinephrine in the synpases between neurons.

They are not used as first-line agents because of their toxicity in overdose and because of some bothersome side effects such as dry mouth, blurred vision, constipation, and urinary retention.

The following tricyclics are currently in the market

Imipramine (Tofranil)

Amitriptylibe (Elavil)

Desipramine (Surmontil)

Nortriptyline (Pamelor)

Cloimpiramine (Anafranil)

The tricyclics were commonly used before the advent of the SSRIs in the late 80s and are effective and useful medications for panic disorder, major depression, and in some cases for generalized anxiety disorder. They have also been used with some benefit for the other anxiety states as well.

The last tricyclic on the above list, clomipramine (Anafranil), has a strong serotonergic effect which makes it a very useful medication for the treatment of Obsessive Compulsive Disorder (OCD).

The tricyclics, as mentioned, cause side effects for some; especially the elderly.

These sideeffects, at the risk of some repetition, are sedation, dizziness, dry mouth, blurred vision, urinary hesitancy and constipation.

The tricyclic amitriptyline is the most notorious for these side effects followed, in decreasing intensity, by imipramine (Tofranil), nortriptyline (Pamelor) and desipramine (Norpramin).

The pupil-dilating effect also poses a risk for exacerbation of narrow angle glaucoma in some patients. At higher doses the tricyclic agents may cause cardiac conduction delays which, when combined with other agents can be a serious concern for causing cardiac arrhythmias.

In spite of the difficulties mentioned, the tricyclics are very effective agents for the treatment of panic disorder and major depression. They are also useful for other anxiety states when SSRI's or SNRI's are ineffective or the benzodiazepines cannot be used due to concerns about an abuse risk.

MAOI's (Monoamine Oxidase Inhibitors)

Monoamine oxidase is an enzyme that causes breakdown of monoamines (serotonin, norepinephrine, dopamine) released at the junctions (synapses) between nerve cells.

MAOIs inhibit the enzyme monoamine oxidase so that the monoamines are not broken down by oxidation. The net result is that there is a rise in their levels.

This increase of monoamine level is felt to be the therapeutic change that is responsible for the efficacy of these agents in the treatment of various anxiety and depressive states.

The problem with their use is that they can interact with other agents that also inhibit serotonin or norepinephrine reuptake, and this can lead to a steep rise of these neurochemicals. This interaction can be lethal.

More specifically, this can lead to a toxic adrenergic response or a toxic serotonergic response. Both of these can be deadly, since the mentioned MAOIs form an irreversible bond with the monoamine oxidase, and there is no way to rapidly reverse their effect.

Due to these potentially deadly interactions, the use of MAOIs is extremely limited and is reserved for special situations where the patient is very diligent about their diet and other medications. It should be reserved for truly refractory clinical conditions with full awareness and consent by the patient of the risks associated with their use.

The prescription should be undertaken with close supervision and follow-up by a seasoned psychiatrist who has experience in the use of MAOIs.

When used, MAOIs have been found to be quite effective for panic disorder, atypical depression, and social anxiety disorders.

Atypical depression is a depressive state marked by increased sleep and increased appetite. This is opposite of the typical depressive states marked by decreased sleep and decreased appetite.

The following MAOI agents are currently marketed.

Phenelzine (Nardil, Nardelzine)

Tranylcypromine (Parnate, Jatrosom)

Most psychiatrists do not want to touch MAOI's with a ten foot pole.

Checking For Drug Interactions

It is useful to check for drug interactions if you are taking more than one medication. Your physician or pharmacist will usually counsel you if there are any serious drug interactions to be aware of. If you want to be extra cautious and prudent, you can check for these interactions yourself at the following website on Drugs.com.

http://www.drugs.com/drug_interactions.html

Cost Of Medication

The cost of medication can be substantial and a limiting factor if brand name agents are used. Medications that are new or brand name can be often quite expensive with their cost running into hundreds of dollars every month. Many medications, however, are also available as generic brands.

The generic versions have good reliability and are equally effective. There is often little to no difference between the generic and brand-name.

Generic medications can be substituted if the cost of a brand-name medication is prohibitive.

Several chains of pharmacies, such as Walmart and Walgreens, offer cards that provide discount rates. Under these plans, many medications are available in 30-day supplies for a nominal charge that is much less expensive.

Other pharmacies have also started to offer such plans which they can afford to do due to their bulk buying of the most commonly prescribed medications. It might pay, therefore, to discuss the cost issue with your local friendly pharmacist. Just be frank and ask if they can suggest a way to lower the cost of medications. They are genuinely sympathetic folks and will go out of their way to assist you with this concern.

Chapter 7

Alternative Treatments

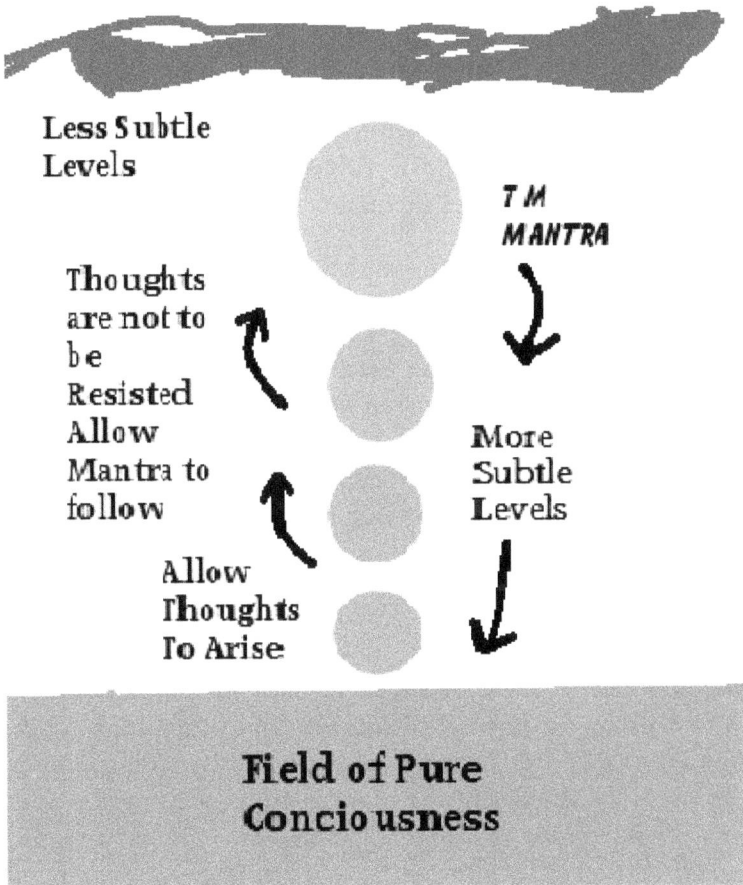

Less Subtle
Levels

Thoughts
are not to
be
Resisted
Allow
Mantra to
follow

Allow
Thoughts
To Arise

*T M
MANTRA*

More
Subtle
Levels

**Field of Pure
Conciousness**

DIAGRAM: TRANSCENDENTAL MEDITATION There
are a number of Alternative or Complementary Medicine

Options available for the treatment of anxiety including Meditation, Yoga, Herbs, Spiritual Counselling, Laughter Therapy, homeopathic medicines, Ayurvedic procedures, acupressure, and others.

These are discussed briefly in this section.

Transcendental Meditation

Transcendental Meditation (TM) is a technique of meditation taught by trained teachers. Training is available in most major cities of the world. In studies, it has been shown to be twice as effective as most other meditations for relieving anxiety.

It uses a mantra given to the student that is private and derived from ancient Vedic sounds.

The technique involves an introductory lecture that goes over the history of the meditation technique. It also goes over the research conducted at reputable institutions of that have validated its benefits. The research is all peer reviewed and based on solid scientific research techniques.

There are certain fees involved and, if the person requests to be taught Transcendental Meditation, a date is set for the formal ceremony. This ceremony is non-religious in nature but is quite enchanting in its formality and somberness. It is marked by the offering of a flower, fruit and a fresh white handkerchief. The Guru in the ancient traditions, or a certified TM teacher in the modern tradition, then invokes ancient scriptures in Sanskrit. At the end, the guru or the certified teacher asks the initiate to chant the last few lines with him or her. At this point, in a state of reverence and calm, the private Vedic sound is granted to the individual.

The teacher meditates with the initiate and answers any questions and receives feedback about the experience from the new meditator. The private mantra is recited silently and, if other thoughts come up, they are not resisted and allowed to come and also allowed to leave. A slight preference is given to returning back to the sound but this is a very slight preference and the mind is allowed to dwell on a thought if it so desires. TM is not a technique of forcible "concentration" or deliberate focusing on anything. Through this nonresistance, the mind gradually settles into more and more subtle layers. There may be periods of no thought and these are beautiful and produce the most rest and rejuvenation. Very interesting and creative thoughts may come up during the meditation and these can be used later if desired but that is not the purpose or goal of the meditation.

A periodic checkup at 1 month and at any other time the meditator wishes is offered as a part of the course.

The benefits of TM are tangible, significant and evident in the lives of those who have used this technique. Many celebrities such as Clint Eastwood, Oprah, Jerry Seinfeld and Dr. Oz and his entire staff attest to it. Schools that have implemented it for their students have seen attendance go up and rates of delinquency drop to record low levels.

TM should be done faithfully for 20 minutes twice a day in the morning and afternoon for the most optimal benefits. A lesser duration can be also be beneficial and better than skipping the meditation.

Nothing should be expected as a precondition when beginning TM. The physiological effects have been well documented. Some interesting changes have been noted in EEG tracings of meditators. During meditation, greater coherence of brain wave patterns between different areas of the brain has been noted.

In order to practice TM, there are no particular religious beliefs that you need to prescribe to. You can, in fact, be an atheist and still benefit from the meditation. It is truly secular and nondenominational.

TM has the potential to increase creativity, productivity and help with the remission of anxiety, depression, and other stress-related conditions. A listing of the studies substantiating benefits can be found at this website.

http://wwv.tm.org/research.html

Finding a TM Teacher: To find a teacher near you, you can call 1800LEARNTM or go to http://www.tm.org

Mindfulness Meditation

This is a technique for being aware and silently sitting with an empty mind without trying to steer the mind in any particular direction. It is a voluntary control of attention to develop a non-judgmental attitude to the flow of experience, perceptions, and thoughts. It has been found useful in reducing pain, provides some relaxation, and may help with some of the cognitive distortions of anxiety. It is recommended to be done for 10 to 15 minutes twice a day.

There is emphasis on not trying to get caught up in the technique but trying to keep it as simple as possible.

Guided Meditation For Relaxation:

In this, the voice of the meditator guides the person through various imageries to achieve a state of calm.

Many of these guided meditations are available for free on YouTube. They can be very useful and do work.

Therapy With Aromas and Flower Essences

Pleasant scents and aromas have long been used to lift the spirits and to create a calming environment. The following oils have been found to be useful for this purpose:

Lavender

Bergamot

Jasmine

Geranium

Cypress

And Sandalwood

Some other exotic scents are also used for therapeutic purposes.

They can be added to a bath, applied to the body, or used in air fresheners.

Naturopathy also offers various flower essences marketed under brand name "Rescue Remedy" that has been featured on the Dr. Oz show and other sites. It is reported to help with stress and anxiety before anxiety provoking event such as taking an exam or starting a new job or enterprise.

Herbs For Anxiety

Hippocrates, the father of medicine, said, "Let food be your medicine." It is indeed true that many foods and herbs can be therapeutic.

Some herbs have been found to have psychoactive properties. They can be effective for anxiety and can be considered if a person does not want to take prescription medications.

Some individuals have a concern about the adverse side effects associated with prescribed medications, and prefer to use herbal and other natural therapies.

It is wise, however, to check with your doctor before you start to take them as some herbs, such as St John's Wort, do have an SSRI mechanism of action and could interact with other medications such as MAOIs.

The passionflower has a MAOI effect and may have potential for interaction. They should not be taken together as they can potentially interact with one another.

The active compounds within the herbal preparations have not been standardized and the purported mechanisms of action are not totally clear for many of the herbal preparations.

They have been found by empirical evidence however to work and offer relief from anxiety even if their exact mechanism of action is not totally clear at this time.

Passionflower:

This beautiful flower was originally discovered in South America but has been cultivated in many parts of the world for its beauty. It contains a psychoactive compound with monoamine inhibiting (MAOI) properties. This compound is concentrated in higher amounts in the leaves and roots. It has been hybridized extensively for ornamental purposes. It produces a state of sedation with benefits for the anxious person. It has been used in tea, and the leaves have been smoked as well. It is also used for insomnia and analgesia for some patients. Because the chemical contained in this plant has an effect of inhibiting monoamine breakdown, a potential toxicity with concurrent use of SSRI antidepressants may occur. This herb therefore cannot be recommended for concurrent use with other antidepressants that enhance serotonin, dopamine or norepinephrine. There are several teas that are marketed under the name passion. Many of these do not, however, contain any passionflower leaves, flowers or roots in them. The label should be read carefully to determine the ingredients.

Passionflower may increase the level of sedation if combined with other sedating agents.

St John's Wort

This herb has been used since the time of Hippocrates to calm anxieties and depressive symptoms.

It has been noted to have mood elevating properties since antiquity. It has been recognized in Germany as a valid therapeutic agent for treatment of anxiety depression and sleep disorders. It is postulated to increase three key neurotransmitters—norepinephrine, serotonin and dopamine. It should not be combined with a MAOIs inhibitor.

St. John's wort has religious connotations associated with it. It was hung over doorways in the medieval period in parts of Europe to "ward off evil spirits".

It may be that the depression, anxiety and malaise that it helped with were the evils that it helped to ward against.

It has been also used as a poultice to decrease inflammation and swelling in musculoskeletal injuries.

It may induce metabolism of contraceptives with lowering of levels of contraceptives. This herb has the potential for causing birth control failure. The women who is taking this herb for anxiety or depression should be aware of this interaction with contraceptive agents.

Chamomile

This herb has daisy like flowers and has been used as a tea for anxiety and insomnia. It has also been used to ease colic in babies.

It should not be used by pregnant mothers as it can stimulate uterine contractions and potentially lead to miscarriage.

Some compounds in this herb have blood thinning properties and may increase bleeding tendencies if the person is already taking blood thinners for medical purposes. Blood thinners are often prescribed to patients who have medical conditions such as atrial fibrillation, mechanical heart valves and sometimes to prevent deep vein clots. Chamomile should be avoided by such patients due to the elevated risk of bleeding complications.

Kava: Kava has been called the natural tranquilizer. The active ingredients are kavalactones and are obtained from the root of the pepper tree (piper methysticum) grown in the South Pacific Polynesian islands. It was used as a ceremonial beverage and was introduced to the world by Capt. Cook and his naturalist colleague George Forster. Kava should not be combined with benzodiazepines or other sedatives. Some cases of fatal liver toxicity have been reported. There is a postulation that it was found in some preparations that had low glutathione levels along with the kavalactones of the extracted compound.

Reishi: (medicinal mushroom): This ancient Chinese remedy has become popular in the United States for reducing anxiety. It is also used to promote sleep.

Ashwaganda: this is an ancient Indian herb that is used for calming anxiety and to reduce stress. Experiments have indicated that it reduces the stress hormone cortisol that is elevated in chronic stress and anxiety.

Green tea: Green tea contains L-theanine, which is found to have calming and soothing effects on the mind. The L-theanine extract is also sold as a separate product in herbal stores such as GNC.

Homeopathic Treatments for Anxiety

Homeopathy is an interesting system of medicine started by a German physician Samuel Hahnemann. He was trained as a traditional physician but was opposed to the then prevalent practice of bloodletting for curing disease. He was a polymath of sorts and later developed the system of Homeopathy in concert with a Viennese physician Anton von Stork.

Homeopathy has been reported to work uniquely well for certain conditions. There are several reputable homeopathic schools of medicine and this form of medicine has a following in all parts of the world.

It is based on the principle that like cures like. This is the principle that if a substance causes a symptom or disease, that same substance in very minute minutes can be used to treat those symptoms. This principle is used when vaccines are used in allopathic medicine but Homeopathy takes the use of this principle to a whole new level.

It is recommended that a medical workup by a regular MD be done to rule out any treatable medical illness that maybe contributing to the symptoms of anxiety. If medical causes have been ruled out, then the homeopathic remedies maybe an option that the person with anxiety may consider among the other options that are available.

Importance of Not Being Biased

We must not be biased against this form of medicine because we do not understand the reported mechanism of action. Understanding as we know well in medicine may come much later than the empirical evidence that a remedy is effective. This is well exemplified by the bark of the cinchona tree being effective for malaria and the foxglove plant being useful for heart ailments even when we did not understand mechanism of action.

Names of Homeopathic Medicines

The following homeopathic medicines are used for the various anxiety conditions. It is useful to be familiar with the names of these medications and what they are indicated for before your meeting with the homeopathic doctor.

Aconitum napellus: This is used for Panic Disorder.

Argentum nitricum: This is used for performance anxiety and social anxiety

Arsenicum album: This is used for people with obsessive compulsive traits and perfectionistic tendencies. It is also reported to work for anxiety marked by pacing and anxiety that is somaticized.

Homeopathy has a peculiar penchant for identifying idiosyncratic symptom clusters. This compound is reported to be effective for "panic attacks around midnight or very early hours of the morning". (These can be symptoms of congestive heart failure or sleep apnea and a medical consultation should be done to rule these out). Patients with excessive concerns about their physical health (hypochondriasis) are also reported to benefit.

Calcarea carbonica: This is reported to work for fear of heights and claustrophobia. It is reported to help with overwhelming stress caused by physical illness or from being overworked. The individual who is getting overwhelmed and sinking into an irritable depression is reported to benefit from this as well.

Gelsemium: Another homeopathic medication indicated for public performance, difficulties with concentration before a test, or before any stressful event. Some PTSD related symptoms such as fear of being in crowds are also an indication.

Ignatia amara: Indicated for a person in grief who is anxious.

Kali phosphoricum: This is indicated for symptoms of anxiety, depression and feeling unable to cope due to overwork or illness.

Lycopodium: Reported to work for the person that is anxious and "lacks confidence". Also reported to work for anxiety that causes digestive symptoms and for claustrophobia.

Natrum muriaticum: Reported to help with Social Anxiety Disorder and symptoms of avoidant personality disorder.

Phosphorus: For the person who is sensitive to criticism and is overly involved with others. It also helps with symptoms suggestive of dependent personality disorder.

Pulsatilla: Also for dependent, clingy individuals who require excessive assurance and support from others. It is reported to also help with premenstrual anxiety and dysphoria as well.

Silicea (also called Silica): For individuals who are conscientious, perfectionistic, anxious and devoted to detail yet never sure of themselves.

Homeopathy Dosages

These are set by the level of their dilutions. Therefore the 30X is diluted 30 times and is more potent than the product diluted only 6 X or six times.

Stores and websites that sell these homeopathic remedies recommend starting with the lower strengths of the homeopathic medicine selected for the symptom. This is usually the 6X or 6C (They mean the same thing). A dose is taken and if the symptoms improve, a second dose is not given until the symptoms reappear again. Sometimes a single dose per day is reported to be sufficient.

Importance of Consultation with a Homeopathic Doctor:

If you are thinking of homeopathic treatment, it is prudent to consult a trained expert instead of experimenting on your own. The above information can give you a starting point for your discussion with homeopathic doctor if you decide to explore this option.

Humor and Laughter As Treatment For Anxiety And Depression

Humor and laughter generated by any means, such as comedy shows, books, plays, TV serials and movies, have been reported to be helpful for anxiety and depression. In his famous book, *Anatomy of an Illness*, Norman Cousins describes how he got better after developing a serious illness and was given a grave prognosis. He checked out of the hospital and into a hotel "where the food was better" and spent time watching funny and humorous movies. He describes in vivid detail the benefits of laughter and humor and recounts how his illness improved by giving way to laughter. There is good reason to believe his recovery was indeed aided by therapeutic benefits of humor and laughter. Laughter does involve the activation of the vagus nerve and there may be other neurobiological correlates that, at this time, are not well defined. This does not mean, however, that they do not exist. The benefits experienced by Professor Cousins and many others are real and deserve our attention and consideration.

Good humor is a tonic for mind and body. It is the best antidote for anxiety and depression. It is a business asset. It attracts and keeps friends. It lightens human burdens. It is the direct route to serenity and contentment.

Grenville Kleiser

Yoga For Anxiety

An ancient method of exercising both the mind and body, and thus helping to relieve anxiety, is yoga. The word is derived from the Sanskrit word which means "to unite" or "to join"— the idea being to harmonize a person's physical and mental potential and unite one's individual self with its source in nature. Yoga, along with the practice of meditation, has been shown to alleviate numerous physical and psychological ailments, including anxiety. In the west these days, the main emphasis of yoga is on the physical postures and movement of the body. Many of the yoga stretches and positions place heavy emphasis on symmetry and maintaining one's balance. A key tool in achieving this is directing attention to your breathing. In doing this, we refocus ourselves on the rhythmic regularity of our bodies. The more we are able to regulate our bodies, the more we feel capable of regulating our thoughts. If we are able to regulate our thoughts, we are then able to manage our anxiety to an extent. This, along with meditation, can be an effective means of relieving stress.

Yoga is wonderful in that anyone can do it. The exercises

may vary from the simplest and most natural of poses (The Child's Pose) to much more advanced positions requiring a more practiced skill (Headstand).

Yoga practitioners also seem to achieve stillness and calming of the mind through stretching and different sustained postures of the body. As mentioned, here are the different types of yoga varying from the still shavasana, or resting pose, to more physically demanding positions of the body. The most popular form is a system of physical exercises called Hatha Yoga.

Yoga emphasizes breathing techniques that may stimulate the vagus nerve, which has been known to also decrease anxiety and depressive symptoms.

Yoga also emphasizes clear thinking and this may also help in avoiding cognitive distortions.

There are various poses or "asanas" in yoga where the student maintains the different positions for set periods of time. The duration is usually a few minutes.

When beginning a yogic exercise, you always begin standing feet together with the hands folded in front of the chest. You gradually begin to engage every part of the body, first centering your attention on the head, neck, and trunk and gradually involving the upper and lower extremities while stretching. The Warrior One and Warrior Two poses, for example, require that we engage and strengthen our core in order to extend the arms and legs for a longer period of time. Deep breathing helps oxygenate the muscles during the more difficult stretches and allows us to hold the positions longer, thereby exploiting the full effects of this very beneficial exercise. It is best to inhale through the nose and exhale through the mouth; however, breathing entirely through the nose has been said to provide the most efficient oxygenation. Breathing deeply is beneficial in that it also engages the core to help further strengthen our posture. Improving our physical posture is reflected in our emotional "posture", so to speak. If we feel we have the strength to stand tall physically, we feel we can stand taller emotionally, be it at work, with family, or in a relationship. The essence of what yoga provides is balance and a mirroring of our minds and bodies. Improving one helps the other.

The following poses have been recommended for anxiety and depression

1. Lotus Position: Sitting cross legged with palms up. There is an emphasis on slow, rhythmic breathing in all the different poses.

2. Viparati Karana Pose: Done near a wall. Lie on your back, arms at your side, with feet up on the wall to make the legs vertical. Assume a restful pose; do regular, calm breathing.

Religion And Faith For Anxiety

Faith and religion can be a wonderful balm for the soul and a great source of strength and healing.

The spirit of tolerance and acceptance should be emphasized by the religious counselor. The more rigid and orthodox fire and brimstone styles can cause more anxiety in the individual. A true religion should provide hope without threats of damnation or bribes of various sorts.

There is virtue in the scriptures of every faith for they are truly inspired. They speak of faith, of doing good for your fellow man and of being patient, tolerant and loving. There is something virtuous of a God who forgives and is ready to accept you as you are.

Many people find it comforting to recite the serenity prayer when they are feeling anxious or distressed. This prayer has been found by many to be useful in sorting out their minds and ridding it of unnecessary worries.

THE SERENITY PRAYER:

"God, grant me the serenity (peace) to accept the things I cannot change; the courage to change the things I can; and the wisdom to know the difference."

This prayer has elements of CBT and problem solving therapy in it.

The original Serenity Prayer was written by Reinhold Niebuhr in 1951. He was a man of deep intellect and had an abiding faith in God. He was a realist, however, and advocated a pragmatic approach to dealing with the difficulties of modern life.

Other Religions:

Lessons about accepting life's ups and downs with equanimity and faith form the cornerstone of all major religion and can provide peace and comfort for the faithful.

Pastors, priests, and other clerics can offer life's wisdom and spiritual guidance based on the religious texts of their individual religions. They should avoid shaming or blaming the individual that comes to them for treatment or counselling.

Every religion promises redemption and forgiveness and this can be of great comfort to the individual beset with needless and exaggerated worries.

Sikhism is a pacifist and tolerant religion that I am familiar with since I was born into it. It was founded by very kind and tolerant man called Nanak and later called Guru Nanak Dev.

The title Guru means a giver of light and it is a honorific given to a person of knowledge and wisdom of a deep spiritual nature. Dev comes from the same root as Divine. It is useful to study Sikhism and other religions. They have some very profound words of wisdom and peace bejeweling their sacred texts.

The Sikh Prayer

God is One

His Name is True

He is the Doer of All Things

He is without fear

He is without enmity

He is formless, He is deathless

His knowledge and His Peace is achieved

By Grace of the Guru

Always Remember

That This Has Always Been True

From the Beginning

It is True Now

And It Will Always Be True
For Ever More

Sri Guru Granth Sahib

(Holy Sikh Book)

Explanation of the Sikh Prayer:

In this prayer Guru Nanak Dev declares to the whole world the benign loving nature of God. It came to him spontaneously after he achieved enlightenment. These are his first words in the enlightened state and the words have been revered as the Original Secret. This prayer is recited to soothe worries by declaring that God is in control and acts without malice or enmity. The prayer is an encouragement to the faithful to accept God's wisdom and purpose. It affirms that God never intends harm for anyone. It is also a consolation and an exultation about the permanent nature of His Goodness.

Popular Preachers

There are many popular preachers that may carry a message of hope for others in midst of their anxieties. Joel Osteen is one such pastor and has a simple style of communication that appeals to many.

He has authored some wonderful books that use the principles of Cognitive Behavioral Therapy. He has published the books as audiobooks in a very clear, kind, and supportive voice. His genuine goodwill and affection for people is evident throughout his discourses. Some of the books of his that are very useful for the anxious individual are as follows.

Every Day a Friday

Become a Better you

I Declare ; Your Best Life, Now

Break Out ; Your Best Life

The spiritual truths that are mentioned cut across different cultures and religions and can be enjoyed by all.

Some other pastors people have found inspirational are

Pastor Rick Warren

Pastor Paul Begley

Pastor Ravi Zacharias

Pastor Joyce Myer

Pastors from other religious faiths can also be equally effective in providing emotional and spiritual guidance for those in distress.

Faith as Strength

If you are a man or a woman of faith, you should hold on to your faith with all your might during times of tribulation. It is the rock that will keep you safe in a sea of emotional upheavals.

Faith can provide you with strength and grace to overcome setbacks and losses. The scriptures promise a comfort and assurance that surpasses understanding. Keep your faith strong no matter what the world may say. Allow it be your great armor and shield in a world that can sometimes be capricious.

Surgical Interventions For Anxiety

Anterior Cingulotomy

Many are surprised to learn that surgery has a role in the treatment of some resistant anxiety states. It is especially useful for a specific type of anxiety disorder called Obsessive Compulsive Disorder (OCD) when all else has failed.

This surgery on the brain, called anterior cingulotomy, is performed at certain advanced medical centers such as the Neurosurgery department of Massachusetts General Hospital and at other elite institutions around the world. To recapitulate, the reasons for neurosurgery referral are intractable cases of the following clinical conditions.

1. Obsessive Compulsive Disorder (OCD)

2. Intractable chronic depressive disorder

3. Intractable pain associated with chronic anxiety, depressive disorders.

4. Other chronic anxiety states not amenable to treatment

OCD is a difficult anxiety disorder to treat and sometimes only marginal benefits can be achieved with medication and psychotherapy. Chronic and severe depression can also pose similar challenges. Surgery can provide significant relief in such situations and is performed by neurosurgeons after they have been screened by many specialists. The surgery itself is called anterior cingulotomy and involves creating an incision or cutting the fibers connecting the frontal lobes and the structures underneath. It is safely performed by lasers under MRI-guided three-dimensional imaging. The benefit of this neurosurgery is apparent soon after the procedure in most cases. At times, a waiting period of 6 to 12 weeks is required for the benefits to be realized and for the symptoms to decrease.

Deep Brain Stimulation

This surgical procedure involves insertion of electrodes for periodic stimulation of different areas of the brain. This technique is still considered experimental and has not been approved by the FDA for treatment of anxiety or depressive disorders.

Deep Brain stimulation has, however, has won FDA approval for treating essential tremor, Parkinson's disease, and involuntary writhing movements known as dystonias.

Vagus Nerve Stimulation Device

The FDA approved the use of a vagal nerve stimulation (VNS) device made by Cyberonics, Inc. of Houston, Texas, in 2005 for the treatment of depression. The surgery involves the implantation of a pacemaker-like device in the chest wall that generates a stimulus. The stimulus is carried to the vagus nerve through thin wires that run under the skin and are woven around the vagus nerve in the neck. The patient is not conscious of the device after it is implanted.

Some patients have been treated for treatment-resistant intractable epilepsy with the vagus nerve implantation device with good effects.

There is also evidence that it is also helpful for the treatment of anxiety disorders. As an aside, vagal nerve stimulation has also proven to be useful in chronic heart failure and movement disorders.

One of the side effects may be a brief hoarsening of the voice if the person is speaking during a period of vagal stimulation. Most individuals learn to adjust their lives around this and often get good at compensating for any such alteration of voice patterns.

Stimulation of the vagus nerve has been found to be helpful for alleviating depression and anxiety. A patent for treatment of depression with a vagus nerve stimulation device was granted by the FDA on July 15, 2005. Further studies were published in 2008 that provide evidence that the VNS (Vagus Nerve Stimulation) Device is also helpful in the treatment of anxiety disorders.

Nonsurgical Stimulation Of The Vagus Nerve

It is interesting to note that the vagus nerve can be stimulated by nonsurgical means as well. It innervates many muscles and is involved in the coordination of a number of complex activities. The following list of actions and activities elicit electrical activity and activation of the vagus nerve.

1. Cold water on the face (Diving Reflex)

2. Singing, Whistling (multiple muscles of throat, larynx innervated by the vagus are activated.

    Perhaps the folk wisdom about the shower with cold water and singing in the shower has some merit after all. It may make for happy days by helping to prevent and treat both anxiety and depression.

3. Swimming exercises all the major body muscles and the exercise is certainly therapeutic for the anxious mind. It may also provide additional benefits via vagal nerve stimulation as a result of contact with water at a temperature lower than body temperature. The coordination required for breath holding in swimming also activates the vagus nerve. If vagal nerve stimulation is valid as a theory, which it seems to be, then a daily swim may be helpful in alleviating symptoms of anxiety and depression. Taking a lap or two around the pool maybe more therapeutic than simple bathing.

4. Diaphragmatic Breathing or deep breathing that is undertaken in some yoga practices may work by stimulating the vagus nerve. Physiologically, this occurs due to the stretching of alveoli walls and activation of the Hering Breuer reflex that sends stimuli via the vagus to the brain breathing centers. Voluntary deep breathing for limited periods can therefore have therapeutic benefits.

5. Laughter Therapy and Laughter Yoga have gained popularity in the last few years. The individuals engaged in these therapies report life-changing benefits from the therapy. The therapy may derive its benefits from activating the vagus nerve.

Laughter has been advocated as the best medicine and there may be some truth in this.

On a philosophical level, laughter has a defiant quality to it in the face of fear and anxiety. It announces with boldness that we are not afraid, no matter what may come our way.

When engaged in any of these activities, it is useful to find a quiet place where one is not likely to be distracted by others. If these activities are performed on a regular basis, they can theoretically help with depression and anxiety via activation of the vagus nerve. One could take a few deep breaths several times a day. One could sing while driving or in the shower or wherever it is convenient. A person could whistle while they walk or do other activities. A person can use their creativity to try some of these methods of stimulating the vagus nerve in a natural way. These ideas and actions may seem out of the box, but they have the potential for making you feel better.

Individual Anxiety Disorders

In the following sections; the treatment of individual anxiety disorders is discussed in more detail.

Chapter 8

Social Anxiety Disorder

This picture shows a young man and woman with social anxiety disorder. They both appear self-conscious and ill at ease. They are not alone, however, due to the fact that social anxiety is surprisingly common.

Social Anxiety Disorder (also known as Social Phobia) refers to a feeling of awkwardness and excessive fear of being judged by others. The individual with social anxiety disorder is mortified by the thought that he or she will be found wanting or deficient in some way by others.

This condition may also be marked by excessive fear of being in social situations. Anxiety is often related to the fear of not being able to communicate adequately and being perceived in a negative manner by others. This can become a self-fulfilling prophecy where the person is unable to communicate due to their anxiety about communicating. Once this happens, they tend to ostracize themselves. They may become more self-conscious subsequently and the hurdle can seem that much greater.

To put it another way, this condition is a fear of being scrutinized by others and found wanting. At other times it is a sinking, panicky fear of being embarrassed and performing poorly in a public event such as a talk, speech, musical performance, athletic demonstration or some other such event.

Clinicians distinguish social anxiety as either being generalized or specific to some of the situations mentioned above.

The good news is that social anxiety disorder can be treated very effectively with psychotherapy and medications.

Treatment Of Social Anxiety Disorder

The treatment of social anxiety usually involves medications, individual therapy, group therapy, and social skills training.

Serotonin reuptake inhibitors (SSRIs) such as paroxetine (Paxil) have become the mainstay of pharmacotherapy for social anxiety disorder. Individual supportive therapy and Cognitive Behavioral Therapy can provide social skills training and clarification of any cognitive distortions. Group therapy is especially helpful as it allows the person to practice their social skills and experience their social anxiety in a controlled, supportive setting of the group.

Prevalence: At any point in time, about 5 percent (estimates vary from 3 to 7 percent) of the US population suffers from social anxiety disorder. Their level of anxiety is above the normal level of anxiety that occurs before a performance or when meeting new people. Social phobia can be of two types, generalized or situation-specific.

Treatment Options: Social phobia symptoms can be decreased by the following interventions.

1. Teaching of social skills

2. Teaching of conversational skills

3. Correction of any obvious cosmetic flaws. Plastic surgery and cosmetic dentistry have done miracles for individuals who have a cosmetic blemish that they are truly self-conscious about

4. If the perceived cosmetic blemish is due to a body dysmorphic delusion, surgery should be avoided and the correct treatment may involve the use of SSRIs or low dose antipsychotics or both

5. Cognitive Behavioral Therapy has been found to be useful.

6. CBT uses two therapists who conduct a group of 4 to 6. Cognitive distortions that occur in social anxiety are discussed. The participants are encouraged to interact with each other. The groups are conducted on a weekly basis and meet for an hour or two at a time.

Practice of social skills in group or in one on one situation can help. It must be repeated multiple times until it becomes second nature in order to relieve anxiety.

Being Present Exercise:

This is an exercise of just being calm and comfortable in the present moment and looking at another person without twitching or looking away. You are allowed to blink if needed but must resume the looking in a calm way without glaring or becoming self-conscious. One can practice this with a friend or a family member. At first it may feel awkward but, when done daily for 3 to 5 minutes for a period of 4 to 6 weeks, it can be useful in decreasing anxiety and self-consciousness.

The purpose of this exercise is not to make you stare at people for a long time; that will just be creepy. The intent of the exercise is to get you over the initial hesitation of looking at someone because of your self-consciousness.

When you can be present comfortably in your own skin in the present moment, you can begin to interact with confidence. This exercise shows you that you can be present and look someone squarely in the eye without becoming anxious. With practice, you will become more confident and more at ease in your interactions.

On the issue of eye contact, the following are considered the norms.

During talking, make eye contact 1/3 of the time that you are talking.

When listening, give more eye contact, for about 2/3 of the time.

For normal conversations, the duration is about 3 seconds to 4 seconds at the most.

Medications For Social Anxiety Disorder

If the person only has social anxiety around specific events, such as giving a speech, then one-time use of a benzodiazepine such as lorazepam half to 1 mg or Inderal 10 to 20 mg half an hour before the event may be useful.

For the more generalized, pervasive kind of social anxiety, the use of SSRIs is recommended.

SNRIs such as venlafaxine have also been found to be useful for social anxiety disorder.

MAOIs should be avoided because there is a long list of medications they can interact with. If other medications are ineffective, and if the patient is highly motivated to comply with the diet, and the doctor checks for foods or medications that the MAOIs may interact with, a trial of these agents can be offered.

They should not be used if a SSRI has been used in the last 6 weeks and no SSRI agent should be used for six weeks after discontinuation of a MAOI. These times are a bit extra conservative but they are safer. These guidelines are more conservative than what is generally recommended but I feel it is better to be safe than sorry when it comes to preventing adverse drug interactions.

Two main interactions that are dangerous and can occur due to interactions with other agents are:

1. Hypertensive Crisis

2. Serotonin Syndrome

Both can be deadly. They can be avoided by avoiding the dietary foods and medications that are banned with the use of MAOIs.

Other Strategies for Treatment - Resistant Social Phobia

At times, combining a SSRI or a SNRI with a low dose of a benzodiazepine such as clonazepam or lorazepam may be helpful in further decreasing symptoms of social anxiety.

When some relief has been obtained, it is important for the person to test out the waters by attending some social functions. As confidence grows, the person may expand their social circle and interact with more people. This combines the benefit of exposure therapy with the benefits of the medications.

Some other medications that have been tried for social anxiety disorder include gabapentin and pregabalin.

These agents are sometimes considered when an individual has issues with substance abuse disorder and benzodiazepines pose some risk for drug dependence.

Although an early response to SSRIs and SNRIs has been noted within 2 to 3 weeks, a time period of 4 to 6 weeks should be allowed for the full beneficial response to be gauged.

If the benefits are not seen in 4 to 6 weeks, the dose of medication can be increased and another waiting period of 3 to 4 weeks should be allowed for further benefits to accrue and reveal themselves.

Once relief is obtained, it is recommended that the individual stay on the medication for at least a year.

Other therapies, such as individual therapy, social skills therapy, and group therapy, should continue even after the initial remission of symptoms has been noticed. This allows for long-term recovery from social anxiety.

It is important for the treatment to continue for at least six months to a year in order to allow for exposure and extinction and desensitization to occur in group settings and for social skills to be incorporated into the natural repertoire of the person's way of relating to others.

Another benefit of continuing Cognitive Behavioral Therapy is to teach the person lasting skills for discriminating erroneous and distorted perceptions and thoughts. In another words, the person gets better at thinking in the right way with time.

In fact, a person should begin to expect that others will act preoccupied or distressed on any given day and that it will have nothing to do with them. They should begin to cultivate empathy and sympathy for the other person that maybe juggling multiple concerns at any given time. This serves to take the focus off the person with social anxiety disorder and also helps them to engage the other person in a more meaningful and patient way without becoming self-conscious or distressed.

The most common cognitive distortion that tends to occur in social anxiety disorder is the overvaluation of other people's opinions and minimization of one's own value and worth.

If depressive symptoms coexist, as is common with anxiety disorders, the SSRI and SNRI medications that are effective for social anxiety are also first line medications for the treatment of depression as well.

Psychotherapy, such as supportive therapy and CBT, will also provide help for current depressive symptoms in addition to preventing future episodes.

The same cognitive distortions that cause anxiety also tend to cause depressive symptoms and the person learning to deal with the distortions in anxiety can apply the same principles to the distorted perceptions of their self-worth and thus remedy the cause of their depression as well.

Chapter 9

Generalized Anxiety Disorder

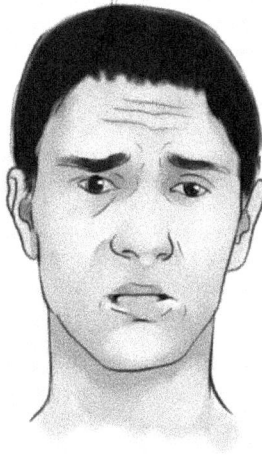

The picture in this section is of a man beset with excessive worries. He has an anxious, worried look with a furrowed brow from constant worrying and the neck and facial muscles seem to be taut. He may in fact be suffering from Generalized Anxiety Disorder.

Generalized Anxiety Disorder (GAD) is a condition marked by excessive worry

and anxiety on more days than not for a period of six months or more. Individuals with GAD often find it difficult to control their excessive worrying despite efforts to do so.

Generalized Anxiety is often accompanied by three or more of the following symptoms: feeling keyed up, insomnia, fatigue, difficulty with concentration, irritability, and muscle tension.

The individual may complain of a headache or neck pain because of the sustained muscular contraction caused by continued anxiety. These aches and pains often tend to come at the end of the day when the muscles are exhausted and tired.

Another sign that may be easy to notice is that when you shake the hand of this anxious person, you may notice that their palms are cold and clammy or moist from perspiration.

Sometimes, the person may engage in nail biting due to anxiety and may have stubby fingernails.

The worries of the person with generalized anxiety disorder are seemingly about mundane things that would not ordinarily bother a normal person to such a degree.

As an example, even if the individual is financially stable and wealthy, they may excessively worry about unforeseen circumstances that may impoverish him or her.

Prevalence of Generalized Anxiety Disorder:

In Europe, studies have indicated a prevalence of GAD in about 2 to 3 percent of the population. The prevalence rate in the United States is a somewhat higher rate of about 4 to 5 percent. The rates of generalized anxiety disorder tend to be lower in countries with economic stability, where people have a way to realize their goals and when they have stable family structures.

Risk Factors for Generalized Anxiety Disorder

1. Genetics: There appears to be a genetic linkage as rates of generalized anxiety disorder tend to be higher in blood relatives of patients with GAD.

2. There is also evidence to suggest that the intelligence of individuals with GAD is generally higher than the average person.

3. The rates of Generalized Anxiety Disorder tend to be higher in those who have been exposed to traumatic events or abuse in their childhood.

Physical symptoms associated with Generalized Anxiety Disorder are listed below.

Insomnia

Headaches

Increased heart rate

Pain in the neck, shoulder, back

Fatigue and difficulty relaxing

Hyperacidity and dyspepsia

Various aches and pains that do not have a clear medical explanation

Tremor

Sweaty palms

Palpitations

Difficulty with concentration when anxiety is severe

Medical Conditions Associated With Generalized Anxiety

The following medical conditions tend to occur more frequently in individuals with high anxiety. These are

- Irritable Bowel Syndrome

- Peptic Ulcer Disease

- Hypertension

- Increased rates of coronary artery disease

Medical Conditions That Can Cause Anxiety

Following the general rule for all psychiatric conditions, generalized anxiety disorder should be diagnosed only when medical causes are ruled out. So here are some medical causes to look out for as they can cause anxiety.

Hyperthyroidism or over-activity of the thyroid gland

Anemia

Stimulant medications

Any respiratory distress

Any conditions causing chronic pain cause anxiety

Any of the other conditions and medications listed under medical causes of anxiety in the initial chapter

Prognosis Or What Happens in GAD:

Although generalized anxiety disorder (GAD) tends to have a chronic course, most individuals learn to overcome and master their anxiety symptoms. With assistance, their recovery can be accelerated and enhanced.

Anxiety is love's greatest killer. It makes others feel as you might when a drowning man holds on to you. You want to save him, but you know he will strangle you with his panic.

Anais Nin

(Prolific Spanish Cuban Woman Author)

Common Cognitive Distortions In GAD

These are as follows:

Catastrophizing: In this type of thinking error, the patient makes a mountain out of a molehill and thinks that the sky is falling based on minor setbacks.

Over estimation of risk: In this situation, the individual over reads minor issues and exaggerates the risk that they might pose.

Perception of not being able to cope: This is common in individuals with generalized anxiety disorder. They can be taught that they do have the skillset to cope with any eventuality that might come up.

Procrastination: This is delay in taking action due to a feeling that one needs more information to make a decision even when enough information exists to make that decision. The persistent need for extra evidence and consistent delays can be a sign of excessive anxiety. The patient can be taught to begin working with what they have and not aim for perfection but learn to accept that good enough is adequate in many situations.

Attentional Bias: With this distortion, the person may pay extra attention to any negative events even though it may not be relevant to their concerns.

Avoidance behaviors: The individual may avoid undertaking projects that they need to do because of anxiety about being criticized or not being perfect.

Treatment Of Generalized Anxiety Disorder

Individuals with generalized anxiety disorder tend to be intelligent, insightful, and take naturally to Cognitive Behavioral Therapy. They may also benefit from training in progressive muscle relaxation and the other therapies discussed in this book.

An approach sometimes taken by some therapists is to expose the patient to a worst-case scenario.

In this, the patient is asked to imagine a worst-case scenario for 20 to 30 minutes. At this juncture, with the help of the therapist, the patient is asked to generate different strategies to cope with the imaginary threatening scenarios.

After doing this, many patients find significant relief and have a newfound confidence and conviction that they will not be totally helpless in their imagined worst-case scenario. As a result of this exercise, the individual may feel more able to handle any negative events that may come up in the future.

GAD anxiety symptoms may wax and wane over time. If a patient finds that their anxiety symptoms have increased for a brief period, it should not be taken as a relapse or a treatment failure but a minor lapse.

Individuals with generalized anxiety disorder are good at imagining the worst-case scenarios and could turn a minor lapse, through cognitive distortion of magnification and catastrophization, into a belief that they are that *one* patient for whom nothing works.

They should be encouraged to analyze their cognitions to rule out any exaggeration or catastrophizing that they may be doing. The correct interpretation of the events can bring reliable relief whenever anxieties start surging again. They should be educated about this and asked to test out this strategy when the next surge of anxiety comes up.

Although Cognitive Behavioral Therapy can help correct cognitive distortions, it needs to be followed by repetition and practice of the lessons learned.

It can be hard to let go of old habits, even if the logic of adopting a new approach is evident to the individual.

With practice of skills, new found success and further encouragement, the individual can learn to grow into a more tranquil state of being.

Medications For GAD

SSRI medications have been found to be effective for treating generalized anxiety states. Paroxetine in one study at doses of 20 and 40 mgs was studied. Both the doses were more effective than placebo - (62 and 68 percent response versus 46 percent for placebo).

The initial dose of SSRI should be increased at 4 weeks if there has been no response. If there is still no response after another 4 weeks, a different SSRI trial is recommended.

If there is still no response, a SNRI such as venlafaxine-extended release is offered. Venlafaxine should be used in low doses to start with and an extended release formulation is preferable to avoid side effects of gastric irritation that are more common in the immediate release venlafaxine.

Benzodiazepines: These medications are effective for generalized anxiety disorder. They are generally not abused by some risk does exist for those with a prior history of substance abuse. The benzodiazepines should never be combined with alcohol or other sedatives as respiratory arrest and death can occur due to potentiation of sedating effects of alcohol or other sedatives.

For the treatment of anxiety, a benzodiazepine such as clonazepam (Klonopin) 0.25 mg one tablet can be used by the clinician once or twice a day to start with. It has a long half-life and builds over a period of 7 to 10 days.

The dose may have to be titrated up initially and then tapered down after a week or so due to the effect of cumulation.

The Risks of Cumulative Toxicity (with long acting medications)

Cumulation is the successive rise of the level of a drug when it takes a long time to be excreted. The length of time it takes for a drug to excreted is measured by Half Life. Half Life is the amount of time it takes for the half of drug to excreted from the body.

When a medication has a long Half Life of greater than 24 hours, it means that some of the drug is still there when the next daily dose is given. This leads to successive rising of levels with resultant rising of effects and sideeffects.

For a long acting sedative such as clonazepam, diazepam or chlordiazepoxide (all of which have long half-lives greater than 24 hours), the successive rise of levels at the beginning days of treatment will require the dose to be adjusted downwards after a steady state is reached.

What is a Steady State?

The steady state is reached in about 4 half-lives when the amount of drug excreted is equal to the daily dose given. After 4 successive half-lives, the effects and any sideeffects should remain stable without further changes. At this point of course, we will lower the dose to an appropriate range where the desirable effect of anxiolysis is achieved without the annoying sideeffects of sedation. This is the art and skill of medicine to some extent.

Clonazepam has a long half-life of 30 to 40 hours. This means that the levels will continue to rise for about 160 hours or about 6 to 7 days. The half-life in the elderly may be longer due to decreased metabolic capacity.

Diazepam can be started at 2.5 mg or 5 mgs once a day. It also has a long half-life and there may be a similar risk of cumulative rise of levels of the medication requiring reduction about a week to ten days out if the side effect of sedation is experienced.

Lorazepam 0.5 mgs two to three times a day is utilized for management of anxiety symptoms. It has a moderate half-life, and requires less metabolism by the liver.

The caution with all benzodiazepines is the risk of sedation. Therefore, driving or operation of machinery should be avoided if the person is feeling sedated or sleepy.

If benzodiazepines have been prescribed daily for two weeks or more and have to be discontinued, the discontinuation should occur by a gradual taper of 10 to 25 percent per week to two weeks to avoid rebound anxiety symptoms.

Buspirone (Buspar) is used for the treatment of generalized anxiety disorder. It does not have side effects of sedation and does not pose a risk of abuse or diversion and many patients prefer it for this reason. Many individuals give up on this useful medication prematurely, without realizing that it takes about two to three weeks before the beneficial effects of decreased anxiety become clear and evident.

The dosage should be started with 10 mgs by mouth twice a day and should be brought up to 15 to 20 mgs by mouth twice a day in about a week. A period of 2 to 4 weeks should be allowed before deciding whether it has provided some relief or not as it takes a few weeks for the benefits to emerge. If the response is insufficient, the dose can be raised to 45 to 60 per day in two divided doses.

Buspar is sometimes used as an adjunct medication along with a SSRI or SNRI agent for the treatment of anxiety or depression.

Pregabalin (Lyrica): This agent works by stabilizing the neuronal membranes. It has been shown to be more effective than placebo in several randomized controlled trials and has earned the approval for treatment of anxiety in Europe. The dosage can range from 50 to 300 mg. Some side effects related to pregabalin may include sedation and dizziness.

Mirtazapine (Remeron) has been used as an augmenting agent with SSRIs or as a stand-alone agent for the treatment of anxiety with insomnia.

Duration Of Pharmacotherapy And Psychotherapy

It is recommended that, once benefit is achieved, the pharmacological treatment and psychotherapy should continue for at least 12 months. This allows for consolidation of psychotherapeutic gains. It allows the healthier cognitive approaches that the patient has been taught to take hold.

After this period, periodic check-ins will be helpful in providing a booster benefit for the therapeutic gains made earlier.

In regard to Generalized Anxiety Disorder symptoms, a quote from the ancient Greek philosopher Epictetus is apt and appropriate.

"Man is not worried by real problems so much as by his imagined anxieties about real problems"

— Epictetus

Chapter 10

Phobias

Arachnophobia

(Phobia of Spiders)

Phobias are intense fears of an animal or a certain situation.

If we look at some of the common anxieties that people have, it is possible to see the logical evolutionary reasons for their existence. Some of these reasons are examined in the following paragraphs with their possible evolutionary benefit.

Fear of heights: During our evolutionary past, falls were associated with injury and death. Any injury, if it was not life ending, still put the person at a disadvantage in the struggle for survival. Injury from falls or any other reason was feared. To be fearful of heights was ingrained in us when people noted that those who disregarded the laws of gravity met a quick end. Defiance of this fear of heights also achieved an unconscious mark of courage. This is the reason perhaps that certain professions such as fighter pilots, airline pilots and stewardesses carry a certain glamour to their professional roles.

Fear of animal bites: Many animals such as snakes, spiders, and scorpions have deadly venoms and poisons which could be lethal to the person. It was natural therefore for a person to be afraid of such animals.

Such vestigial ancient fears have become magnified in some individuals and lead to the development of phobias to snakes, spiders and bugs.

Fear of large predators: This fear needs no explanation. An interesting offshoot of this fear, however, is the fear of clowns with big heads. The large heads that clowns often have for the purpose of caricature may invoke vestigial evolutionary anxieties about large predators that also have big heads such as lions.

Separation anxiety: This is related to the primitive fear of being isolated from one's pack. Human beings evolved as communal pack animals. We have survived over the ages by working together, being supportive of one another and offering protection from the vagaries of starvation and predation. There was strength in numbers and belonging to a group offered this in exchange for loyalty and support for the group. When isolated, due to being separated or lost, we were extremely vulnerable on the open savanna.

Fear of starvation: This may be related to some of the eating disorders as there was a great need to conserve food. Anorexic states and bulimic states may be twisted manifestations of these fears.

Claustrophobia, Agoraphobia: This is related to fear of being unable to escape. As mentioned before, being alone and vulnerable was a primal fear in our past. Women may have been even more vulnerable and this primal fear may be higher in them. This may be the reason that agoraphobia and panic disorder states exist in higher rates in women even today.

Fear of Darkness: This may be related to the fact that most predators are active at night and have better night vision than human beings. It made sense for human beings to be fearful of the dark and stay within their caves. This enhanced fear of the dark may be the reason darkness is still associated with sinister or dangerous things; for example, the phrase 'dark motives' comes to mind. The fact that darkness was associated with all things sinister may be a reason that dark-skinned people were felt to be somehow dangerous.

By being more enlightened about these factors, we can look at these primitive fears objectively and be more rational about our perceptions. The pigmentation of the human skin from being dark to light is related to the amount of sun exposure that is present in the area where people evolved.

Human beings who evolved in areas where sunlight was more oblique, as is the case in higher latitudes such as Europe, had lighter skin pigmentation in order to absorb more ultraviolet rays in order to form vitamin D. In areas where sunlight was more direct, such as in the equatorial regions, the pigmentation was darker in order to block excessive penetration of ultraviolet rays that might be damaging to the skin while allowing enough to form vitamin D.

For this reason, dark-skinned people are more vulnerable to vitamin D deficiencies than lighter-skinned individuals.

So as you can see, phobias are the distortions and exaggerations of some common fears.

Let us take a look at some of the treatment options available for their treatment.

Treatment Of Phobias:

Phobias are diverse and can develop about any object, animal, or situation.

The treatment for phobia is primarily through exposure, desensitization, and Cognitive Behavioral Therapy.

Medications have a limited but useful role and can be very helpful for specific situations.

When the situation that precipitates phobia is rare, medications such as benzodiazepines are given only for the short term to help the person get through the difficulty.

For example, if a person has a phobia about flying they may take a low dose of benzodiazepine such as Lorazepam half to one mg or Clonazepam in a similar dosage. These individuals should not combine the medication with alcohol as the sedating effects can be enhanced and can be dangerous.

There may be other specific phobias during which such short term use of medications may be helpful. There is risk of sedation and the person should exercise due caution if operating dangerous machinery or driving.

SSRIs such as Paxil, fluoxetine or Prozac have been found to have some benefit over placebo in treating phobias. Some interesting anecdotes of benefit for specific phobias with certain SSRIs are also noted. An example of this is a case report of an 11-year-old boy with storm phobia who found relief with fluvoxamine.

The best treatment approach often is one where the use of an SSRI is combined with exposure therapy.

Some interesting reports have been generated about the use of a corticosteroid hydrocortisone about an hour before exposure therapy.

When the corticosteroid is combined with exposure, the benefits are greater than when exposure therapy is carried out alone and by itself.

The exact mechanism of how this occurs is not clear. Corticosteroid use after a traumatic event has also been linked with decreased rates of development of PTSD.

When treating phobias by desensitization, the exposure to the agent that induces phobia can be done in real life or through the imagination.

When exposure is done through imagination, the patient is guided and asked to hold an image of the feared object. They are gently guided to approach in their imagination the feared object step-by-step.

In real life exposure, the feared object is at first placed at a distance and the person is asked to gradually approach within 10 feet, then 3 feet and through incremental steps to ultimately hold or touch the object with their hand.

An example of imagined hierarchy is as follows:

1. Say the word spider

2. Look at a picture of a spider

3. Touch the picture of the spider

4. Sit 5 feet away from a plastic toy spider

5. Hold the toy spider

6. Watch a video of a spider

7. Watch a spider in a container

8. Hold the container containing the spider

9. Allow the spider to come out and walk away

Exposure by virtual-reality is another way to provide exposure therapy. In this procedure, a helmet projects in front of the eyes a realistic recreation of the feared situation.

Building A Resilience To Anxiety

In order to build resilience to anxiety, we must understand that ups and downs occur in everyday life. They are a part and parcel of existence and cannot be avoided.

Having accepted the fact that change is constant, everyone can benefit by developing skills that help us to adapt to any change that might come our way.

One of the basics of survival is the willingness to adapt and to change. Once we adopt this mindset, we are never going to be overtaken by surprise and will be less anxious as a consequence. Change may actually bring good things our way and not all change is bad.

Being adaptable may put you at the helm of the situation to take advantage of the opportunities it provides.

Very few things are set in stone, except for such things as the cardinal principle of avoiding harm to others.

You should also remember all the times that you have successfully adapted in the past. This should give you courage and confidence for the future.

Being confident is half the battle won when it comes to dealing with anxiety problems.

Resilient people believe in themselves and their ability to overcome, adapt, and cope with any difficulty that might come their way.

Resilience can be taught by teaching people how to problem solve and develop alternative solutions to any setbacks. People under stress often develop a tunnel vision where they are unable to see alternatives. Resilient people see alternatives in every situation and do not get stymied by failure or setback.

They are incurably optimistic and not afraid to ask for help. Their willingness to ask for help is a sign of strength and they also see it in this way.

Resilient people also have a sense of purpose to their lives and know why they want what they want.

Resilient people adapt but never give up.

Chapter 11

Panic Disorder

This is a picture of a man in an acute distress during a panic attack. The panic attack is marked by a rapid surge of anxiety that peaks over a span of 1 to 2 minutes. The sufferer can be bewildered and in a state of fear for their life.

Panic Disorder is an anxiety disorder that is marked by surges of anxiety that last 10 to 15 minutes. The anxiety can be overwhelming and the person may feel that they are going to die. In addition to the intense anxiety about physical safety, there may be an intense fear of losing control of one's mind. There may also be a sense of not being able to catch one's breath and an overwhelming sense of doom. The patient is taken to the emergency room where extensive workups are not helpful in revealing any underlying medical disease.

This is frustrating for a patient with panic disorder who believes he or she is suffering from an undiagnosed heart problem or other serious disease.

Panic Disorder, however, is not lethal and no one dies of a panic attack. The person, however, is not assured and fears the next attack when he or she is certain they are going to die. When the person survives multiple such episodes, they are able to accept with a sigh of some relief that perhaps they are not going to die when the next panic attack comes. This is the beginning of the cure for panic disorder.

Initially however, the person can develop a secondary fear of being in public places from where escape from embarrassment caused by a panic attack is impossible. This is called agoraphobia and leads to a housebound existence for such individuals.

Some symptoms of acute panic attacks are as follows:

Heart palpitations

Fast heart rate, hyperventilation, tremulousness, restlessness, dizziness, feeling faint along with a sense of bewilderment and acute anxiety.

In order to diagnose Panic Disorder, some of the following criteria should be kept in mind:

1. There are recurrent panic attacks

2. At least one of the panic attacks has been followed by anxiety for a month or more. The anxiety often is about having additional attacks. Sometimes the anxiety centers around the consequences of the panic attack.

3. These panic attacks are not the result of intoxication or withdrawal from a substance and are not due to a medical condition. Furthermore, they are not due to another psychiatric condition such as phobias or flashbacks of PTSD.

Sometimes the panic attack occurs in a limited manner wherein the symptoms are fewer and milder in intensity. This is called a limited symptom attack.

A significant number of people may have a limited symptom attack or one isolated episode and not develop a panic disorder. They generally do not need to be medicated.

Ruling Out Medical Disease In Panic Disorder

A medical illness may produce panic like symptoms: When the panic attack occurs for the first time, a full workup is recommended. This is done to ascertain the cause of the acute symptoms reported by the individual.

It is vital to rule out any medical causes that could be related to the myriad symptoms reported during a panic attack.

Some of these conditions are as follows:

Hyperthyroidism with a thyroid storm

Cardiac arrhythmias

Toxic levels of stimulatory medications such as theophylline

Tyramine reaction in patients on MAOIs

Coronary Artery Disease

Pulmonary Embolism

Pheochromocytoma

Temporal Lobe Epilepsy

Epileptic foci in other areas of the brain such as the frontal lobes

Coronary artery disease usually implies a narrowing of the arteries supplying blood to the muscle of the heart. This narrowing is caused by deposits of fat plaques on the inner lining of the blood vessel (atherosclerosis).

Ischemia means that there is not enough of an oxygen supply to the heart muscle because of the arterial narrowing.

Angina is the chest pain experienced because of the heart muscle being choked of oxygen by the narrowed arteries. A medication, nitroglycerin, is usually prescribed in the dose of 0.4 mgs to be placed under the tongue for relief of the angina chest pain. It works by dilating the blood vessels and allowing more of the blood supply to reach the heart. The long-term management of narrowed coronary arteries is done by the cardiologist or cardiac surgeon by coronary bypass surgery or balloon angioplasty to open up the narrowed arteries.

Sometimes a piece of the inner fat plaque may break off and drift downstream into a narrower part of the coronary artery causing an acute blockage of all blood supply. This may lead to death of the muscles downstream of the muscle that is deprived of the oxygen. This death of a part of the heart muscle is called myocardial infarction (MI) and is a serious event. It is also called a heart attack and the individual is usually hospitalized in the ICU for closer monitoring.

Arrhythmias sometimes develop after the initial recovery from the heart attack and need to be treated with medications or a pacemaker. The cause of the arrhythmia is the damaged heart muscle which is more irritable and likely to send off errant action potentials (cell membrane stimuli).

In order to rule these out, certain investigations are carried out in the ER. Pulmonary embolism and other respiratory causes may require imaging studies to rule out any pathology or active disease process pertaining to the pulmonary system.

Any heart arrhythmias can be ruled out by conducting a 24-hour monitor recording of the cardiac rhythm. This may not always detect the erratic and unpredictable onset of certain arrhythmias but it does provide greater assurance than a single EKG strip.

Attacks of angina and myocardial infarction produce specific changes on the EKG. These changes on the EKG are not found in Panic Disorder attacks. Rest and nitroglycerin usually relieve the pain of ordinary angina, but the pain from a myocardial infarction is not easily relieved by rest or nitroglycerin and is more severe and intense in quality.

If any muscle cells die due to infarction, the enzymes within those cells are released and these are checked by laboratory assays. The enzymes checked are <u>creatine</u> phosphokinase (CPK mb), creatine kinase (CK), and the proteins troponin I (TnI) and troponin T (TnT). Laboratory monitoring of the cardiac enzyme levels is done within an hour of arrival to the ER, at 8 to 10 hours after symptoms onset and at 24 hours. If there is no elevation of the cardiac enzymes, a myocardial infarction can be ruled out. Panic attacks due to Panic Disorder do not show such elevation of the enzymes.

The investigation of the adrenal tumor pheochromocytoma is somewhat more cumbersome. It involves the collection of a 24-hour sample of urine and measurement of the catecholamines in the total sample. Catecholamine (metanephrine) assays may also be done in the blood. If abnormalities are found, ultrasound and MRI imaging may be ordered to detect any increase in size of the adrenal glands.

In order to diagnose pheochromocytoma, the 24-hour urinary metanephrine levels are checked. When the level is more than two times normal, imaging studies with a MRI of the kidneys is ordered.

The core of the adrenal gland is called the adrenal medulla. It normally produces stimulatory excretions called catecholamines. These are namely norepinephrine, epinephrine, and dopamine. A tumor of the adrenal medulla is called a phaeochromocytoma. The tumor provides a greater number of cells to generate these secretions, resulting in a higher production of the stimulatory compounds.

The diagnosis of this tumor was rare in the past but with the easy availability of detailed imaging by MRI nowadays, more cases of pheochromocytomas at greater frequency than before are being recognized and treated. When the tumor is surgically removed, the problems related to the sudden surges of anxiety and related bodily symptoms also begin to rapidly subside.

If any neurological issues are suspected, a brain wave study or an electroencephalogram (EEG) may be ordered.

When all of these conditions have been ruled out, the patient may still feel that their panic symptoms are caused by some undetected medical problem. They are hesitant and resistant to the idea that their panic symptom is related to a psychiatric condition and are certain the doctors are making a big mistake in not locating the medical cause of their severe symptoms.

The Psychological Causes Of Panic Disorder:

Panic attacks tend to come out of the blue by definition in Panic Disorder.

We all know, however, that most things don't just come "out of the blue". We are just not conscious of where it came from and that can become the job of psychotherapy. It is a job for both the patient and the therapist.

Even if no specific stressor is noted at the time of the panic attack, it has been found that the overall level of stress is higher in the lives of individuals who suffer from panic disorder when compared to the rest of the population. There may have been a number of incidents in their earlier life that were adverse and over which they had no control.

This event may have been damaging to their sense of security, their sense of self, and their self-esteem. A significant loss, such as the death of a spouse or a parent, may also be noted in their past social history.

The causes of panic disorder are often unclear. There are theories proposing that the person has suppressed or repressed many of their fears and anxieties and that at times such anxieties bubble through the veneer of stability.

Treatment can often be targeted towards these unstated fears, and exploring the options to handle these can often then be therapeutic.

Genetic Causes Of Panic Disorder:

First-degree relatives are likely to have panic attacks or other anxiety disorders.

Childhood Abuse:

A history of childhood abuse or neglect is found to be more common in the histories of patients diagnosed with panic disorder.

Prevalence of Panic Disorder:

About 2.7% of the population at any time has symptoms of panic disorder. The incidence in women is almost twice as much as in men. This implies that about 5 % of women may experience panic attack symptoms at some time in their life and about 2 % of men may also experience a panic attack.

Dysfunction Due To Panic Disorder:

The individual may become fearful of the next panic attack and some people start to avoid being in public. They fear being embarrassed or ridiculed by the public when they are having such attacks.

If avoidance is severe, it can interfere with their ability to carry out their jobs, in addition to restricting their social life.

Stigma With Panic Disorder

There is a sense of shame about their condition among patients with panic disorder, as is the case with other anxiety disorders as well. This may limit getting support from family or friends.

The revelations by some celebrities of their own struggles with anxiety states such as panic disorder have served to decrease the stigma to some degree.

One of the other reasons for the delay in finding psychiatric help is the repeated pursuit of medical causes of their condition. It is with disbelief that they come hesitatingly to the psychiatrist.

Coexisting Conditions:

Stress from untreated panic disorder can lead to clinical depression, agoraphobia, and abuse of alcohol or illicit substances. The latter is often a misguided attempt at self-treatment.

Depressive illness, alcoholism, or substance abuse issues are very treatable. It may be necessary for the detoxification to occur prior to a full assessment of the anxiety state.

Medications for control of panic disorder symptoms can be started as soon as the detox is complete.

The benefits of medications are evident in the first month in most cases. In other cases, a titration of the dosage maybe needed.

As with other anxiety disorders, the role of Cognitive Behavioral Therapy in sustaining recovery and remission can never be overemphasized.

The medications used for panic disorder often treat any coexisting depression. Support from family and the treating doctor and assurance that effective treatments exist can provide hope to the patient.

With the remission of the panic attacks, depression and despair also begin to lift. With continued remission, a person can regain confidence and their poise again. As they resume their regular roles again, it is important for them to make lasting lifestyle changes to decrease the overall stress level in their lives.

Complications Of Panic Disorder:

An uncommon complication of panic disorder is the anxiety between panic attacks and the development of phobia about being in open spaces. Because of the intense symptoms involved, the person may become fearful of having a panic attack in public where they may be viewed by others and from where escape to a safe sanctuary may not be possible.

This leads to the development of secondary fear of open spaces or public places where escape from public embarrassment would be difficult. This fear of open or public spaces is called agoraphobia.

Agoraphobia is also an independent phobic disorder and may occur in the absence of panic disorder.

Course:

It has been found that about 60% of the patients who are diagnosed with panic attacks or panic disorder achieve the remission of their symptoms in about 5 to 6 months.

Pharmacological Treatment of Panic Disorder:

If no medical cause is found for recurrent panic attacks, a referral to psychiatry is made to rule out panic disorder. Thus panic disorder is a diagnosis of exclusion.

The patient may implore the doctor to keep looking for a medical cause. They can find it hard to believe their symptoms are psychiatric in nature.

Much to their later surprise, the use of medication such as SSRIs can bring relief from their panic attacks.

SSRIs are, for many psychiatrists, the first line agents for panic disorder. The following SSRIs have been found to work.

1. Paroxetine [Paxil]

2. Citalopram [Celexa]

3. Escitalopram [Lexapro]

4. Sertraline [Zoloft]

5. Fluoxetine [Prozac]

6. Fluvoxamine [Luvox]

Starting Treatment:

It is useful to start with lower than normal doses of SSRI medications in individuals with panic disorder or any other anxiety disorder. This is because anxious patients seem to be more attuned to their body and are sensitive to side effects. The dose can be raised after a week to ten days to the normal therapeutic dose. When starting treatment, it is important to explain at the very outset the expected time course of the expected response. Some clinicians also prefer to lower expectations and emphasize that the medications are only part of the solution and that psychotherapy is also an important component. In this manner, they try to ensure that the patient is not discouraged by the lack of an early response.

This allows the body to adapt and avoids side effects that may turn the anxious patient against a treatment that may be potentially helpful.

The benefits from medications for panic disorder are noticeable in 2 to 4 weeks and continue to increase over the next couple months. If there has been an inadequate or partial response at the end of 4 to 6 weeks, an elevation in the dose of the medication is recommended.

SNRIs are also utilized and are effective but may have higher rates of gastrointestinal side effects such as nausea. If venlafaxine is used, the blood pressure should be monitored at visits as there may be a small risk of the elevation of blood pressure at the higher doses. It is prudent to check for blood pressure elevation and adjust the blood pressure medication as indicated.

When educating about care in the future, it is important to remember and remind the patient that brief setbacks may occur with an occasional panic attack still occurring. The panic attacks, however, are not dangerous and they do get better over time. There is no reason for pessimism or despair. The key is to persevere and keep going. It does get better and the symptoms abate and decrease over time.

As discussed earlier, the panic state is uncomfortable but will not be life threatening.

Write down the words "I have come out of prior panic attacks without dying. This too shall pass." Keep this on an index card in your pocket and read it when a panic attack seems to be coming on.

When your panic attack subsides, after a few minutes, read this again. Stay calm and strong.

Just A Talisman, A Lucky Charm:

Sometimes a token pill of an anxiolytic is carried by a patient, almost like a talisman.

It can be used if needed for severe anxiety. Just the assurance that it provides by its presence is enough to ward off an anxiety attack.

If you are prescribed this, you can use the token emergency medication, if needed. The token medication can often be carried in a small locket or medication vial available at drug stores.

Panic attacks usually remit within 4 to 6 weeks after starting SSRI medications. In a few months, with continued remission, the fear of a panic attack will also be gone.

When the fear of having an attack is gone, the associated fear of being in a public place will also fade away.

Medications called monoamine oxidase inhibitors or MAOIs are also effective as are the tricyclic antidepressants. MAOIs are not used by most clinicians in view of the wide range of drug interactions. They interact with other medications such as, tricyclics, SSRIs and stimulants with life threatening complications.

Tricyclics are not used much as first line agents for Panic Disorder but they are very effective when used. They do have side effects such as dry mouth, constipation, and dizziness that are well tolerated by most patients but may be bothersome to individuals.

They cannot be used in those people with narrow angle glaucoma or urinary hesitancy or urinary retention due to an enlarged prostate.

Sometimes, family members are entrusted to give the medication to the patient to ensure compliance in patients that may have difficulty with compliance.

The tricyclic antidepressant imipramine was one of the first agents that was found to be effective for panic disorder. The benefit for panic disorder is evident within one month of starting imipramine.

Some of the serotonin reuptake inhibitors, or SSRIs, can initially cause some restlessness and anxiety in some patients. It is prudent to start with a low dose for 7 days before raising the dose of the SSRI to the effective range. An excessive zeal on the part of the prescriber can cause more problems than it solves and should be avoided.

Venlafaxine is also an effective medication for the treatment of anxiety and depression. It enhances both serotonin and norepinephrine and can be effective in lower doses than used for depression in the range of 75 to 150 mgs per day.

Clomipramine (Anafranil) is a tricyclic that is one of the most effective tricyclics for panic disorder and for OCD (Obsessive Compulsive Disorder).

Benzodiazepines can be excellent treatments for immediate relief of anxiety and can be effective over the long term as well. Concerns about dependence and abuse are often overstated and not a problem for most people. If a person has a history of problems with alcohol or drugs, they should be avoided and treatment with SSRIs is the wiser course to pursue.

The dietary supplement inositol may also improve symptoms in some people.

After one to one and a half years of relief, patients can consider tapering off their medication gradually while they are being monitored by the treating clinician. If there is a relapse of the symptoms, the medications can be restarted again.

Agoraphobia – A Relic From The Stone Age..?

Agoraphobia is marked by an extreme fear of open spaces. The person often feels that they will be unable to escape from a situation that may be life-threatening. Agoraphobia is more common in women and some have theorized that this is a relic of our stone-age history.

Women were vulnerable to being kidnapped if they were alone as they were a prized "property". In the brutal history of internecine warfare down the ages, the women were not harmed for the same reason.

This may have led to the fear of open spaces such as the savannah or steppe where there was no place to hide and they were more visible. This fear over the eons may have been encoded in our very genes. It may becomes manifest at certain stressful times in some individuals.

This intense fear of open spaces is thought by evolutionary psychologists to be a relic of our stone age past.

Chapter 12

PTSD

A SOLDIER WITH PTSD;

A WOMAN WITH PTSD

These pictures of a man and woman are shown to depict some features of Post-Traumatic Stress Disorder (PTSD). The woman looks perplexed, anxious and has a numbed stare and expression that can be found in survivors of trauma. The man has the uniform of a soldier and has a similar look of emptiness, often called the "thousand mile stare".

Posttraumatic Stress Disorder (PTSD) is an illness that has been around as long as mankind can remember. It has been a tale told in a thousand voices and a thousand ways. These range from the hunts painted on rock walls, to the epic poetry of Homer. In the past two centuries, various names such as soldier's heart, Daccosta syndrome and battle fatigue were given to the same familiar illness that we now call PTSD.

Many times, PTSD is not so obvious and the person may just be thought to be a hermit or a loner. This is because the person afflicted with PTSD may shun company. Any socialization and banter can become a trigger for painful memories and flashbacks of past traumas. Solitude is such sweet bliss for the person for whom every social interaction becomes a potential jab from the past.

In patients with PTSD there is a need to consciously avoid reminders of the trauma. They may not volunteer information about the events that plague their waking experience or color the landscape of their dreams.

They may be perceived by others to be quiet people who prefer their privacy and are just not very emotionally expressive. People close to them may say things like, "He changed after the war. He is just not the same."

At times, some PTSD patients may act out their trauma by actively seeking risky activities and be perceived by others as an adrenaline junkie.

In all of these different states, whether quiet or boisterous, they are often trying to exorcise and remove their inner demons that trauma has somehow implanted deep in their soul.

What Causes PTSD?

PTSD is caused by exposure to life-threatening situations where the person's life or the life of those around the individual was in great peril. They may have been shot at, physically beaten, raped, or violated in other ways, or may have witnessed such misfortune befalling others.

Although life-threatening and traumatic events can occur anywhere, they are more likely to occur in certain special situations. On a battlefield where heavy caliber weapons are used, a person may witness much mayhem, destruction, and loss of life.

Emotional trauma is also more likely at the scene of a violent crime, such as rape, robbery, or organized mob violence.

In cases where the person is a dependent, as in the case of a child, a dependent wife, an individual with handicaps, or an elder, the risk of abuse rises and there may be a greater perception of threat and vulnerability on the part of the dependent person. The rates of PTSD tend to be higher in such situations as well.

The traumatic event that causes PTSD may be a onetime event or may be a recurring situation.

The question of why some individuals develop PTSD while others do not is an interesting line of inquiry. The factors that determine whether someone develops PTSD are complex and not totally understood at this time. There is some conjecture that those with childhood trauma may be at a higher risk for developing PTSD.

After an emotionally traumatic event or accident, it is normal for the person to re-experience the moment and have flashbacks of the event for a period of time.

They may even have nightmares of the event but these symptoms usually subside with the passage of time. If the symptoms are severe but last under a month, the syndrome is called acute stress disorder.

If they last for more than a month, the condition is called PTSD. The risk of developing PTSD is higher if the trauma has occurred chronically or in more than one situation.

SYMPTOMS OF PTSD

Some of the symptoms of post-traumatic stress syndromes are as follows:

Flashbacks of the traumatic event

State of increased arousal and vigilance

Emotional lability and irritability

Emotional numbing and decreased display of emotions

Risk-taking behaviors to challenge fears

Episodes of emotional outbursts marked by tearfulness or physically striking out.

Behaving in response to flashbacks with fear, anger, or cowering in a corner or social withdrawal.

Social withdrawal is marked by lack of close contact with old associates and sometimes contact with family members is also withdrawn.

Amnesia for some parts of the traumatic event has been noted. This may be the mind's natural way of trying to seal over trauma.

Persons with PTSD may feel detached from the environment or the environment may seem unreal.

Self-blame and survivor guilt may be found in in survivors. They sometimes blame themselves and feel guilty for having survived when others were killed.

At times, they may blame themselves for making the abuser act towards them in the way that the abuser did. There are often features of accompanying depression in such situations.

When PTSD symptoms are severe, social and occupational impairment is likely to be found. In order to cope, some individuals may take up solitary occupations such as truck driving or being a forest officer, night-time postal workers, or other such careers. Such vocations allow them to limit contact with others and thus hide their dysfunction from others. Solitary occupations may help them to avoid social triggers for flashbacks of prior events.

ONSET: After a deeply traumatic event, the person often goes into an emotional shock. They may go through a gamut of emotions and different symptoms such as avoidance, tearfulness, flashbacks, nightmares, and fear of the event occurring again.

If this state lasts for a month or more, the diagnosis of PTSD is warranted.

At times, the person may be able to organize themselves and "hold it together" at the time of the original trauma but can have the onset of PTSD much later after an event triggers the release of prior traumatic memories. This is called delayed onset PTSD.

Case Study: Roxana is an immigrant from Serbia. She immigrated with her family to the United States due to the uncertainty of the social situation in the home country. When she received the news of the death of her friend in the home country, a flood of emotions was released including memories that she had suppressed in the past. She became increasingly withdrawn, tearful, and began to startle at loud noises. She began to manifest all the symptoms of a person who had just survived an intense physical struggle. The death of her friend had reminded her of the carnage and death that she had witnessed in her war-torn country prior to immigrating to the United States many years ago.

Prevalence:

In the United States, some studies have indicated a 3 to 5% prevalence of PTSD in the general population. Many individuals who suffer from PTSD do not seek help for their condition and some may continue to function at subpar levels.

Co-Occurring Illnesses:

Rates of alcohol, substance abuse, and depression are higher in individuals with PTSD.

Treatment of PTSD:

PTSD can be treated and symptoms can be lessened with the help of medications and psychotherapy.

Treatment often involves the use of individual therapy, group therapy, and community support groups. If substance or alcohol use are problems, substance abuse groups are also recommended. If detox is needed, this is provided first.

Group therapy has been found to be very useful for decreasing the symptoms and lessening the sense of alienation. Groups can provide support and validation for those who have felt that they would not be understood.

If someone has started to use alcohol on a regular basis, they will need a complete history and physical examination. The laboratory evaluation is also ordered to assess liver function, renal function, a complete blood count and electrolytes.

In addition, it is important to check for micronutrient deficiencies such as B12, thiamine or folate deficiency as alcohol can impair the absorption of micronutrients.

Such micronutrient deficiencies may contribute to anxiety and mood symptoms.

Detoxification from alcohol should be done in a supervised setting. It is done by cross covering with a benzodiazepine such as Librium 25 to 50 mgs three to four times a day and tapering by 20% per day over 5 days. More importantly, the individual should not detoxify from alcohol without supplementing the diet with thiamine to avoid permanent damage to a portion of the temporal lobe involved in memory consolidation.

Damage to this area can lead to a condition called Korsakoff's syndrome. In this syndrome, the person recalls his past memories but is unable to lay down new memories due to damage incurred during detoxification from alcohol. They may make up facts and confabulate to cover their amnesia.

If someone has developed a secondary opioid dependence, this can also be remedied by medically supervised detoxification. The detoxification can be made comfortable with a slow taper and it can be achieved relatively safely.

Cognitive Distortions In PTSD

Some of the cognitive distortions or twisted thinking that occurs in PTSD is around the tendency to personalize and self-blame. Distortions also tend to occur around the likelihood of the reoccurrence, magnification, minimization, and catastrophizing of innocuous situations.

The person pained by survivor guilt may want to consider that he or she is not responsible for the situation and the traumatic event could have occurred no matter what anyone did.

There should be an expectation that most individuals with PTSD will get better with time because most symptoms do decrease over time.

It helps to keep things in perspective and allow the individual to take credit for what they have done right in their life.

Most PTSD survivors are true heroes who have struggled to achieve their goals despite the obstacles that were strewn across their life's path.

Advice For The Sufferer Of PTSD:

If you suffer from PTSD, share your thoughts with your therapist. Keep a diary of your thoughts and emotions. When you're feeling down or need to isolate yourself, make a mental note of what thoughts you are having at that time.

With the help of your therapist, you can examine these thoughts together and look for any cognitive distortions. After these are recognized, the corrective thoughts should be adopted and repeatedly used to replace any distorted cognitions that may try to crop up again.

Try to maintain a regular time for waking and going to sleep and set aside some time for physical exercise.

Anniversaries

Anniversaries are a difficult time for some people. Go over your notes about past cognitive errors and, when these crop up around the time of an anniversary; replace them with the corrective thoughts. Once you gain success in overcoming these "automatic negative thoughts" by replacing them with more "automatic positive thoughts" this will enhance your self-confidence and decrease your sense of guilt. If you can do this, you will never go back to being blindsided by the automatic negative thoughts again.

Some PTSD patients especially find great comfort and solace from their church or religion of choice.

Try to read the scriptures from your religious tradition that give you comfort.

In the Gideon Bible that is often placed for free in hotels and motels, different verses for different emotional states are also mentioned. Reciting these with faith and devotion has a great therapeutic benefit for some individuals. You may want to give it a chance and may be pleasantly surprised by the results.

Being educated about PTSD is helpful. Good psychotherapy is directed at providing education about the causes and reinforcing a corrective emotional view of the situation as not being the fault of the individual.

One should try to repeatedly remind oneself that, with treatment, symptoms can decrease significantly over time and the outlook is not as bleak as it may appear to the person who is in the middle of the emotional malaise that is PTSD.

Supportive therapy to shore up healthy coping mechanisms is encouraged. Your therapist can provide this by listening to you attentively and complimenting you for the positive gains that you have made.

What Friends And Family Can Do

If you are a friend or a family member of someone with PTSD, you can be supportive by validating them as valuable human beings and complimenting them for the positive gains that they have made no matter how small the gains may be.

Psychotherapy Techniques For PTSD

The psychotherapy for PTSD is pursued by a combination of cognitive therapy, exposure therapy, teaching of coping skills, and supportive therapy.

One of the key aspects of a truly healing therapy for PTSD is to allow the person to relive the emotions attached to the trauma in a safe environment. The traumatic material should be processed and the patient should be allowed to bring up details of the event, reflecting as many details as possible. They may be asked to consider if an earlier event had occurred that was similar to this. This is important because the vulnerability to PTSD is based upon some earlier trauma which the patient had healed over but was reopened when the new traumatic event occurred. Oftentimes there are cognitive distortions and misperceptions around the original traumatic event.

The patient is asked to go back and recall the sights, sounds, thoughts, feelings and other facts about the situation. By re-experiencing the trauma through imagination, the valence and the emotional hold that this event has on the person is loosened. When emotions are re-experienced at a deep level in a safer environment and examined, the anxiety that was tied to these emotions not being examined begins to drift away. A courageous look at our traumatic past is the homage that we must pay in order to gain our freedom from such anxiety. If we run away and try to hide, the anxiety will only follow us.

Virtual reality has provided another tool for the treatment of PTSD. By putting on 3D goggles, the person can have an experience of revisiting this original traumatic event in a vivid and realistic manner. The patient is allowed to have whatever emotions come up and told that they are in a safe environment and can discuss and talk about any details that come to their mind. Sometimes certain memories that have been repressed may surge through into consciousness during one of these confrontations with the past. Once these are processed, however, there can be a significant lifting of the negative emotions associated with PTSD.

The Cognitive Behavioral Therapy for PTSD centers on correcting their distorted views about their vulnerability and safety in the current environment. They can be educated and encouraged to become self-aware by a Socratic method of questioning. Through such facilitated introspection, they can regain power and control of their life at this time

They can also become aware of the various conditions in their environment that allow for greater safety than they may have experienced in the past.

Any faulty assumptions and any faulty cognition can be useful fodder for the therapy mill where cognitions are examined and refined.

The patients are taught to modify their thoughts that are not in concordance with the reality of their current existence.

Sometimes traumatized individuals may develop over-generalized beliefs about the world being a noxious and unpleasant place. This can be corrected so that they do realize that other people *do* care and that their emotional suffering can be healed.

Because of their emotional numbing and isolative behaviors, the spouses of PTSD patients may be stressed and the relationship may be strained.

Couples therapy involving the partner and the PTSD victim is, hence, very useful. It improves the communication between them and increases intimacy and trust when the spouse understands what the patient is going through.

Some other therapies that are used in helping with PTSD are the teaching of coping skills, enacting role-plays, and assertiveness training.

Stress management skills and relaxation training such as the progressive muscle relaxation can also help to decrease symptoms. Transcendental Meditation™, yoga, and mindfulness meditation can be great tools to help with stress management. TM has been shown to be more effective than ordinary relaxation techniques. Assertiveness training can help avoid aggressive acting out.

Biofeedback can teach the sufferer to control their emotions by being able to the physiology associated with anxiety. They can view their skin conductance and their brain waves and are taught to control these factors. When they gain control, they can adjust their physiology and brain waves to the pattern that is conducive to a relaxed state of mind. When they can reproduce the results at will, it gives them increased confidence about being able to handle any anxiety symptoms that may emerge in the future. They are not as afraid of flashbacks, and intrusive recollections with the resultant anxiety and dysphoria.

EMDR This novel treatment stands for eye movement desensitization and reprocessing. This treatment has been found to be helpful in some cases. In this technique, the person is asked to relive a traumatic moment while their eyes are instructed to move side to side. This is repeated until the emotional intensity associated with that recollection begins to fade. At this point, the cognitive distortions are clarified, and undistorted views are presented in place of the distorted views. The premise is that the moving of the eyes from side to side may simulate the rapid eye movement of the dreaming state. Dreaming states are thought to be the mind's natural way of trying to sort out traumatic memories. It is for this reason that nightmares are more frequent after a traumatic event in order to process the trauma but gradually recede in frequency.

Expressive Writing Therapy:

In a study gauging the effect of emotional writing, it was found that, when people were asked to write about their most upsetting experiences, they found it difficult at first but, once they started, it became easier. They were allowed to destroy the letter without showing it to anyone. After they had done this, many individuals noted a significant relief of their depression, anxiety and worry.

It appears that the act of writing adds a kinesthetic component to their experience and thereby makes it more real and more cathartic than an ordinary recounting might do for someone. It also stimulates an examination of context and relationship of events to each other. All of this is conducive to "getting it out" and is therapeutic for the individual.

Advice for Cathartic Writing:

The individual should be advised to find a place to write and devote 15 to 20 minutes a day to writing. They should include any painful or hurtful things that may have happened to them in the past and free-write without worrying about editing or grammar. The writing is for them and does not have to be approved or audited by anyone.

In addition to the psychological benefits, a study also found benefits for the immune function in individuals who had tried Cathartic Writing.

Medications For PTSD

Medications for PTSD:

SSRIs such as sertraline (Zoloft), paroxetine (Paxil), fluoxetine (Prozac), citalopram (Celexa) and escitalopram (Lexapro) have been found to be useful in the treatment of PTSD.

The medication should be initiated at a lower than normal dose and gradually raised to the therapeutic dose in 7 to 10 days. This is done to limit initial side effects.

Once the effective dose is reached, you may not notice any

significant improvement for 4 to 6 weeks. It can be frustrating to wait this long but you should faithfully continue to take the medication even if the benefits are not immediately apparent.

If there is no response or insufficient response at 6 weeks, the dose can be increased.

Medications other than SSRIs are also used for PTSD. This includes the SNRI venlafaxine.

Intrusive flashbacks and startle responses begin to respond in 4 to 6 weeks.

If distressful nightmares are a problem, prazosin (Minipress) may be helpful. It is normally used to treat hypertension and urinary hesitancy related to an enlarged prostate. It blocks stimulatory alpha receptors in the peripheral tissues as well as in the brain. These receptors are overactive in the PTSD patients and, by blocking these in the brain; the medication provides relief from nightmares that are felt to be related to the alpha over-activity.

Prazosin is prescribed in a dose of one to two mgs at the hour of sleep (HS). It has been found to be helpful for nightmares in both combat veterans and in those with noncombat related PTSD.

The lower dosage is used initially and due precautions should be exercised when rising as it dilates the blood vessels and can cause dizziness upon arising due to blood pooling in the legs in the dilated blood vessels.

Your doctor may also consider the use of atypical antipsychotics such as quetiapine and risperidone if the symptoms are severe.

The data for the use of these agents in PTSD, however, is

sparse. Their use should be limited if possible to avoid side effects related to metabolic syndrome.

Metabolic syndrome is a condition that occurs with the use of atypical antipsychotics and is marked by elevation of cholesterol, increase in weight, and an elevated risk of developing diabetes mellitus.

Other Treatment Options

Herbals for PTSD have not been well tested. Some of the sedating herbals such as valerian and some of the serotonergic herbals such as St. John's Wort may be beneficial. St. John's Wort should not be combined with the use of MAOI inhibitors as there may be some risk of a dangerous condition called serotonin syndrome.

Transcendental Meditation(TM) and yoga have been found to be very helpful by some researchers for handling anxiety states including PTSD. You may consider learning TM or joining a yoga class.

Outlook for the Future

Many overcome the trauma. You can use it to make you stronger, to make you more resilient. The anxiety may bend you but you can decide to not let it break you.

Like others, you can learn to overcome the trauma, to replace that movie reel, replace those negative automatic thoughts, and take your sacred space back. Like many other survivors, you can go on to have a productive and meaningful life.

Allow your wiser, more compassionate, and more empathetic self to emerge. When you take the first step towards healing, the healing moves two steps towards you. Intention has great power. Make it your intention to get well.

Historical Individuals Who May Have Suffered From PTSD

Florence Nightingale:

In 1854, she served as a nurse caring for British troops in Turkey where they were fighting the Russians. She saw grievous wounds in the soldiers and worked up to 20-hour days in very trying conditions. She developed a near fatal illness herself and, despite being asked to go back to Britain, stayed on and continued to lead as an example of dedication and compassion for the sick and dying. When she did return to her home country, she is reported to have become irritable and withdrawn and exhibited symptoms consistent with PTSD. She recovered later on and continued to be a role model for others.

Captain James Cook:

This intrepid sailor and explorer explored the Pacific Islands, the east coastline of Australia, and the western coastline of the Americas. During his voyages, he witnessed horrific acts of violence, cannibalism, death by sickness and disease, and also lost two of his own children while away. The traumatic events seemed to have taken their toll and, in his later years, he grew cantankerous, profane in his language and rash whereas he had been more measured and moderate in his behaviors before. He may have been rash and provocative in his behaviors with the Hawaiian warriors as well. He was killed by the Hawaiian warriors during one of their meetings.

Some Thoughts On The Prevention Of PTSD

There is some evidence that the use of morphine during traumatic injury decreases the risk of development of PTSD associated with the trauma. Other evidence indicates that the use of corticosteroids such as hydrocortisone during an acutely traumatic event may also provide a protective effect against the development of PTSD.

An argument has been made in some circles that animals that are constantly at risk of becoming prey in the wild do not exhibit the enhanced startle or avoidance behaviors after they've had a close call with being killed. It has been pointed out that they may have a surge of yet unknown neuroendocrine secretions that puts them in a state of hypnosis and detachment when their death is imminent. They supposedly do not feel the pain of their demise either. Some individuals who have had a close encounter of a deadly kind report a similar state of detachment and anesthesia.

This profound state of rest or torpor may be what nature provides as a solace to the victim of a brutal survival game.

The profound states of rest achieved through meditation, such as have been documented with Transcendental Meditation, may provide a similar level of protection against the development of PTSD.

I think we all have blocks between us and the best version of ourselves, whether it's shyness, insecurity, anxiety, whether it's a physical block, and the story of a person overcoming that block to their best self. It's truly inspiring because I think all of us are engaged in that every day.

Tom Hooper

.

Chapter 13

OCD (Obsessive Compulsive Disorder)

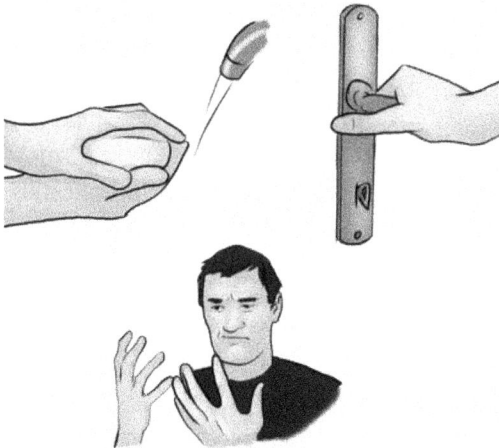

This picture depicts a man beset by concerns about germs on his hands that he tries to wash away with repeated hand washing.

Symptoms of OCD

This disorder is characterized by intrusive thoughts, obsessions and compulsions. The compulsions are acts that the person feels compelled to be perform in a certain way to offset the thought that is repeatedly intruding into their conscious experience. They feel unable to stop the obsessive thoughts. The thoughts can be silly, and are often unwanted and distressing. The person recognizes their thoughts and their behaviors to be irrational. Many feel self-conscious and ashamed of their condition and fear that others will think they are crazy. They try very hard therefore to be discreet as possible about their symptoms.

In the above example, the hand washing may be repeated many times in a day, resulting in severely dry, cracked skin that may even bleed. The more they try to resist, the harder it seems to resist. This can be very frustrating and trying for the person and they adapt by trying different rituals in the hope of decreasing the intensity and frequency of intrusive thoughts. These rituals become the compulsions associated with obsessive-compulsive disorder. These compulsive behaviors can be actions such as tapping something three times before undertaking a task, circling the building before entering it, or repeatedly washing their hands or checking all the locks multiple times.

These behaviors are done to overcome, for example, the thought of having touched harmful germs or to overcome the nagging intrusive thought that the door is somehow unlocked. Even with the rituals, the anxiety is not relieved and it just gets more and more difficult for the person with OCD. Some patients may spend hours in rituals on a daily basis.

Obsessive Compulsive Personality Is Not Obsessive Compulsive Disorder

OCD is different from obsessive compulsive personality disorder. The person with obsessive compulsive personality disorder does not have intrusive and distressful thoughts and does not engage in ritualistic behaviors to assuage their thinking. The person with obsessive compulsive personality disorder, however, is particular in paying attention to details and may have a rigid style of thinking or obsessive need for cleanliness and organization. They generally do well on a professional level due to their high level of organization but may have difficulties in their personal lives unless the spouse understands and works around their unique needs for organization. They usually tend to be very conscientious and are otherwise wonderful human beings.

Prevalence Rates of OCD: The prevalence of OCD in the general population is in the range of 1 to 2 percent of the population. It is therefore not a rare condition.

A Unique OCD Syndrome In Children -"PANDAS"

A unique OCD syndrome can develop in children called "PANDAS" after a strep throat infection. The acronym stands for Pediatric Autoimmune Neuropsychiatric Disorders Associated.

It has all the hallmarks of OCD marked by obsessions, rituals and compulsions. Some children are mortified by the thought of contamination and cannot stop washing their hands.

It is an autoimmune response to the antigens on the coating of the Strep A bacteria that causes strep throat. The proteins have a similarity with the proteins of the basal ganglia of the brain. The antibody that is produced, therefore, by the body to fight the Group A bacteria starts to fight the brain's own tissues in the basal ganglia.

This damage leads to abnormal movements (Chorea or St Vitus dance) and OCD features such as intrusive obsessive thoughts, repeated ritualistic behaviors such as door checking and hand washing.

Factors That May Worsen OCD Symptoms

A. Emotional trauma or stress can exacerbate OCD. Sometimes, new onset OCD behaviors can occur after a traumatic event.

B. During the late luteal phase of the ovarian cycle, i.e., during the premenstrual periods, it can be worse.

C. During the postpartum period after a woman has delivered a baby, there may be an exacerbation of OCD symptoms with a rise of obsessive ruminations.

These thoughts can take one or more of the following patterns:

- Thoughts of contamination

- Thoughts of violence, of harm befalling someone, or someone falling ill

- Thoughts with unwanted urges such as stabbing, spitting, etc.

- Thoughts about symmetry and obsessing over what is not symmetrical or "not right"

- Intrusive taboo thoughts

- Other unwanted and unpleasant thoughts

Normal Coping Strategies in OCD

The normal coping strategies are to avoid and suppress, and when these don't work, to engage in compulsions to alleviate them.

Types of Compulsions

The compulsions in OCD can include the following:

Washing, counting, checking, ritualistic motor behaviors involving a number of steps, repeating words etc.

There may be avoidance behaviors to avoid triggers for obsessive thoughts.

The intensity and frequency of obsessions and compulsions can vary—from one or two per day to being constantly plagued by unwanted thoughts.

Secondary Symptoms: The person may become demoralized by uncontrollable symptoms and sometimes may blame themselves for perhaps wanting these thoughts or of being immoral. What they don't realize is that OCD is a biologically driven illness with neurochemical pathology that can be improved with medications. It has nothing to do with morality or their worth as a person. When their neurochemistry is corrected, their symptoms abate without any lessons on morality.

Tics and OCD

Motor or vocal tics have a higher than average incidence in individuals with OCD. Tourette's Disorder has both motor and vocal tics and many symptoms along the obsessive compulsive spectrum.

Age of Onset of OCD:

- The typical age of onset is about 20 years of age and onset after age 35 is unusual.

- Pediatric OCD beginning as early as age 10 has been noted. An acute beginning is more likely to be associated with an infectious etiology.

- Early age of onset may also have a greater genetic contribution. There is a greater than average likelihood of another blood relative also having obsessive compulsive symptom patterns.

- Hoarding Disorder is a variant of OCD with thoughts of harm befalling if some vital object is thrown away.

Treatment Of OCD:

Obsessive compulsive disorder is a very treatable condition. The patient with OCD is often referred by others and there is great reluctance by some patients to engage in treatment.

Much of this resistance is due to the shame and stigma of their seemingly unusual thoughts and compulsions.

This worry, however, is misplaced because most doctors are familiar with this clinical condition.

The doctors and other clinicians who treat OCD recognize that it is not a weakness or a fault of the person for having this condition.

They also recognize that it is not humorous or funny in any way. The more informed clinicians recognize that OCD is a real illness related to a unique neurochemical disturbance.

The case for biological roots of OCD is stronger than perhaps any other anxiety disorder. Almost no psychotherapy alone works as well as medication such as SSRIs (Selective Serotonin

Reuptake Inhibitors) for the treatment of OCD.

- Medications such as SSRI's that increase the level of serotonin in the junctions between nerve cells (synapses) are very helpful. They are the mainstay of treatment and help to decrease OCD symptoms by a mechanism that is not well understood beyond the fact that they raise intrasynaptic serotonin levels. They have been found by multiple trials to decrease the intensity and frequency of intrusive thoughts and compulsions.

- Some of the SSRIs used for the treatment of OCD include medications such as sertraline (Zoloft), paroxetine (Paxil), fluoxetine (Prozac), citalopram (Celexa), and escitalopram (Lexapro).

- Effexor has also been used with some benefit.

- The tricyclic clomipramine (Anafranil) has been shown to strongly inhibit the reuptake of serotonin and is also effective in treating OCD.

- The time course of response is 8 to 12 weeks; hence the individual should be patient and not expect benefits to occur right away although earlier responses are sometimes noted.

- It is first desirable to choose an SSRI such as sertraline, citalopram or escitalopram because they are less likely to have interactions with other medications.

- Citalopram at higher doses has been associated with cardiac conduction delay and an EKG may be ordered when the dose reaches 40 mgs of citalopram or 20 mgs of escitalopram.

- Sertraline has a higher incidence of side effects related to the gastrointestinal tract such as diarrhea, and nausea. These usually subside after a week or two but it may be simpler to just switch to a different SSRI if these sideeffects are noted.

- The doses of all SSRI and other medications should be begun at the lowest dose and gradually built up to the therapeutic levels. Patients with anxiety disorders tend to be more sensitive to side effects. These side effects are less likely if a lower than average starting dose is chosen. Once a day dosing is better for compliance and this should be chosen whenever possible.

- The final effective dose of SSRI for OCD is higher than the average dose for depression. It tends to be at the higher end of the upper limit.

- Augmentation is sometimes tried with typical or atypical antipsychotics for residual symptoms.

- The atypical antipsychotics such as risperidone, olanzapine and others that block serotonin receptors have the potential rarely of exacerbating OCD symptoms.

- If atypical antipsychotics are used, clinical monitoring should be done by measuring body weight and quarterly metabolic profiles. This is to prevent the emergence of a metabolic syndrome that may occur as a side effect of atypical antipsychotics.

- Metabolic Syndrome can be caused by atypical antipsychotics or obesity due to any cause. It is marked by weight gain, elevation of serum cholesterol, and resistance of the tissues to insulin. The resistance of the tissues to insulin is related to a pre-diabetic or diabetic state.

- If there is any sudden change in the mental status of anyone on atypical antipsychotics such as olanzapine (Zyprexa), risperidone (Risperdal), clozapine (Clozaril, Fazaclo) or other atypical antipsychotics, a stat blood sugar check should be done to rule out very high blood sugar levels. Some cases of sudden diabetic ketoacidosis have been noted with the use of atypical antipsychotics for any cause.

- Cognitive Behavioral Therapy is very helpful for managing distressful obsessions and should be a component of any treatment plan for Obsessive Compulsive Disorder. The distortions that often need to be worked on include the need to be perfect, the magnification of fears, or catastrophizing of situations that the patient finds stressful.

- Cognitive Behavioral Therapy is sometimes combined with exposure and response prevention therapy. This involves exposure to the fear of germs, for example, by shaking hands with another person and preventing the immediate compulsion of washing hands. Some studies have indicated that the use of a medication D-cycloserine while doing this facilitates the extinction response (the fading of the stress associated with the stressful stimulus such as a handshake).

A Multipronged Approach Is Best

The treatment of OCD involves a multi-pronged approach with medications, supportive therapy, support groups, and education about their conditions. Medical conditions that may be exaggerating their anxiety also need to be ruled out.

Be Patient with Medications:

If you or your loved one suffers from OCD, it is important to remember that the benefit of medications may not be apparent for a period of up to 8 to 10 weeks. Hence, one should not get dismayed if an immediate response is not apparent in the first few weeks of treatment.

Some Notable Individuals with OCD traits

Nikola Tesla (1856-1943)

This brilliant scientist delved into many different areas of science such as electricity, radar, radio waves. His inventions in the area of generating electricity changed the course of human history. What is less known about Nikola is his obsessive tendencies that resulted in some odd, stereotypical, and ritualistic behaviors. Based on these accounts, it is believed that he suffered from OCD. He had obsessive and intrusive thoughts that would make him anxious. In order to control these intrusive thoughts, he would do things such as walk around the block three times before entering a building. He also was known to engage in other behaviors such as counting the number of bites in his meal and also keeping track of the number of napkins that were used. He refused to shake hands with others for the fear of contracting germs.

Martin Luther (1485-1546)

This great reformer of the church is said to have suffered from obsessive and unwanted intrusive thoughts that he tried to dispel.

Thomas Stonewall Jackson

The Confederate General was given to obsessions and various intrusive thoughts. Among other things, he obsessed about whether his arms were equal in length. His obsessive attention to detail in military matters may have contributed to his legendary skill as a tactician and for being a dogged fighter.

Howard Hughes (1905- 1976)

This famous billionaire, filmmaker, and aviator also displayed symptoms related to OCD. He carried a huge fear of germs and isolated and secluded himself in his later years. He also developed complex and strange behaviors such as eating only a certain kind of food for stretches of time. He also scattered objects around the room in a certain way and forbade others from talking to him or interfering with his mental life. He died a recluse due to his self-imposed isolation.

Bonus Chapter 14

Testing Anxiety

Everybody has to take a test at one time or another. Some have to do it more often than others and this can be a significant source of stress and anxiety.

It is normal to be anxious before an exam. Some amount of anxiety can be a good thing and it can help us to focus and concentrate better. High anxiety, however, can be detrimental. This chapter will offer you some useful tips to keep the anxiety within manageable levels.

The keys to reducing test-taking anxiety are the following logical and straightforward steps.

1. Give yourself enough time to review the material two to three times before the test.

2. The first time, don't worry about remembering or memorizing, just focus on trying to understand the big concepts.

3. Look at any notes you took during the lectures and see if there was an emphasis laid by the professor or teacher on a particular topic. It might be important to memorize the important facts related to that topic.

4. If there is a question bank that explains the answers, go over it.

5. Make it a point to have a schedule and try your very best to stick to it.

6. If you stick to the schedule, you will not have time to worry about anything else.

7. Sticking to the schedule will simplify the planning element and take that anxiety out of the equation.

8. It will be simple as just putting one step in front of the other or following the schedule hour after hour, day after day. Just do what is scheduled and everything else will take care of itself. If you are not able to finish a scheduled topic, make a note of it and keep going to the next scheduled area of study. You can come back to it later.

9. If you have other stressors or worries on your mind, it is important to discuss them with a confidante, close friend or, if available, a therapist.

   If you cannot find a therapist, you can confide your worries to a trustworthy friend or family member and accept any assurance or help that they provide.

   Rituals and prayers provide comfort and support to some people and, if you are a religious person, you should consider incorporating this into your routine.

10. A conversation with a therapist can sometimes be life changing. We sometimes set ourselves up to fail because we think that is what we deserve or what is expected of us. There are negative, abusive persons from the past who may have set those expectations. Because you could not fight them at the time, you may have unconsciously adopted their mindset in line with the survival strategy of "If you can't beat them, join them."

He or she may be afraid of disagreeing with the oppressors who told him or her that they would always fail and never succeed. With courage and clear thinking, and with or without the help of a therapist, you can rewrite that script and decide to be courageous and succeed although it "feels more right" to fail. You can choose to thumb your nose at all your detractors.

11. By becoming aware of any such unconconcious life scripts, you can erase them and write new ones that predict success and a contented life for you.

There may be underlying fears of being judged and a fear of failure that can paralyze efforts for success. The fear of failure can thus can become a self-fulfilling prophecy. The key is to never give any mind to what others may think of your success or failure. Decide to pursue all efforts in order to satisfy yourself and for no one else.

If you have a history of abuse and suspect you're your abusers are still affecting your ability to succeed, you should consider talking to a therapist about this. With the help of the therapist you can start working on solutions to overcoming any self-defeating behaviors

238 | Overcoming Anxiety

that are fulfilling your feared abuser's prophecies. Decide to be totally liberated and free of their noxious influence from the past.

Take practice tests. It will help you to get used to the real life experience of the test and will improve your score. This will help you to be more relaxed when the real test day comes.

Think of practice tests being similar to shooting at basketball hoops before a basketball game. Practice can reveal very useful ideas that will help you when you take the real exam.

Classes Offered By The School For Exam Taking Techniques

Many schools offer classes on test taking strategies. Find out if your school offers any classes or guidance on test-taking. If offered, take full advantage of them. By participating in them, you are also showing the school that you take your studies seriously and they also feel vindicated (thanks to you) for having arranged for the classes in the first place. It's a win-win situation.

Creating A Study Strategy:

It is a well-known fact that, in order to prepare for a test, you need to determine the number of days you have before the exam. Then divide the subject to be studied into different sections; assign different days and blocks of time to each section.

Try to have two rotations of such reviews; on the second go around, try to go over the same material faster in a shorter time block of time.

Post the schedule prominently and try to stick to the schedule. If you slip up a bit, don't worry, just continue with the plan and stay faithful to the schedule and study what is allotted to the next block of time.

Set enough time to review the subject two to three times. At each review, try to go over the sections that you have reviewed at a faster pace. Recollect details you have remembered before as you go through the second and third review.

Make It Multisensory

Try to get as many sensory organs involved in learning as you can. Try to write out the information (kinesthetic), hear it (auditory) and see it (visual). Most people are highly visual so it helps to review diagrams and create your own diagrams whenever possible. They don't have to be elegant works of art, but clear enough for you to recognize what you are depicting.

Maintain good sleep hygiene, and get regular amounts of some exercise. This maybe a brief walk as you recapitulate the information you just learned.

Visualize and Walk Your Success

When you walk or jog around the block, make it a meditative experience and visualize yourself succeeding. Hear the congratulatory words; feel yourself winning; see yourself being satisfied and even exulting in your success. See yourself confident in the knowledge and taking the exam successfully.

You can do this with any form of exercise. At other times, visualize your knowledge before you as you walk or engage in any other ordinary activity.

When thinking about the test, always picture yourself doing well on the test and remove any images of you stumbling on the test and not doing well. Imagine the positive scenario upon arising and before going to bed.

Live a Healthy Life

Maintain regular and healthy nutrition. Avoid overeating due to anxiety. Take a multivitamin pill with minerals during the period, especially if you don't have access to regular healthy meals that you might ordinarily prepare.

Learn some relaxation techniques such as the progressive muscle relaxation technique.

Learn meditation techniques such as Transcendental Meditation. It has been shown by studies that it can improve your focus, concentration, and problem-solving skills.

If You Have ADHD (Attention Deficit Hyperactivity Disorder)

ADHD is neurological condition present since childhood that leads to difficulty completing tasks that require sustained attention. It was originally thought to resolve itself by the mid-teens. Modern day demographic surveys, however, have revealed that the ADHD syndrome continues to persist in varying degrees in adults about 30 percent of the time if it has been present in childhood. The adult form of ADHD is called ADHD residual type.

ADHD adults are creative and unconventional in their approaches in many areas of their lives. They may not, however be so good at sustained attention that is required in preparation for an exam.

The duration of some exams also poses a challenge for the ADHD adult even if they know all the answers. They may become impulsive and rash and jump to conclusions without thinking through the whole question that is being asked of them. Thus, without treatment there are hurdles in the preparation and the taking of the exam for such individuals.

If you do have ADHD, and are undergoing treatment with medication, you should continue on your regular dosage.

If you suspect you have ADHD but have never been treated, you should ask for a consultation with a psychiatrist or a psychologist who deals with the assessment and treatment of this condition.

The criteria for ADHD residual type have undergone revision in DSM V. It recognizes that many individuals, despite having had symptoms of ADHD in childhood, were never offered treatment. The clinician can use other collateral information to establish the diagnosis of adult ADHD.

For the treatment of this condition, there are pharmacological and nonpharmacological strategies that can be used.

Some benign nonstimulant medications that can be safely administered for its treatment are guanfacine (Intuniv). Atomoxetine (Straterra) has also been found to be useful by some but it carries a rare risk of hepatotoxicity that can be fatal.

The stimulant medications used for ADHD are many and diverse. They should be used only under the supervision of a doctor. Possession of them without a prescription is illegal and serious charges can result if these are passed to anyone else.

Stimulants when properly prescribed for a valid ADHD

242 | Overcoming Anxiety

condition are not harmful and can make a significant difference in academic performance and in the personal life of the individual for the better.

According to the data that has been studied, a person with ADHD will not abuse the stimulant medications.

The stimulant medications should not be used by a person without ADHD for the mere purpose of getting an edge or for pulling an "all-nighter".

If you don't have ADHD, the stimulants will not be helpful and can cause side effects such as anxiety, tics, fast heart rate, and insomnia. Other severe side effects include activation of mania or psychosis in the vulnerable individual. The use of stimulant medications, therefore, should not be undertaken lightly.

An Indian Auyrvedic herbal preparation called ashwagandha is claimed to help in coping with stressful situations of any kind. Some people have reported benefits in memory, retention and focus during exam times with this herbal preparation.

Look At the Sample Tests

If you have a sample of the test you are taking, be sure to look at the sample test questions. If you can practice on the test *under exact simulated test conditions,* it will be very helpful. You can use a stopwatch or other device to keep you within the real-life test parameters of the exam that you will be taking.

By practicing and getting decent scores on the practice exam, you will not only enhance the chances for your success, but reduce your test anxiety as well.

On The Day Of The Exam

On the night before the exam, try to get at least 5 hours of sleep. Even if you are awake, you can lie in your bed, keep your eyes closed and let allow any thoughts to come and go and just be there. If you do not open your eyes for 45 minutes but just allow the mind to free float, you will find yourself going to sleep. The hardest part is keeping the eyes closed but, if you do this, you will be able to get some deep rest. You can take a sleep med if you are prescribed this to facilitate sleep onset.

Have two sets of alarms 10 minutes apart, if it is an important exam. Try to get and up and start moving to awaken faster once the alarm goes off.

On the day of the exam, get to your test center at least half an hour early so that you don't have to worry about getting there on time.

When the Exam Starts

Read the questions carefully.

When you have finished the first 10 questions, take a few deep breaths and do this at an interval of about every 10 questions.

This will allow you to relax and also allows your brain to rest. Test taking is a very cerebral activity and your brain nerve cells are at their peak metabolic levels during test taking. Your brain will perform better with a brief rest of 45 to 60 seconds every twenty minutes or so. You will be better focused and able to problem solve in a more nimble manner.

The deep breaths serve to oxygenate the blood stream to

optimum levels and exhale the accumulated carbon dioxide excreted by the active brain.

If you come across a difficult problem that you can't figure out, mark it, come back to it later and don't waste too much time on it.

Go on and solve the remaining problems that might be easier for you and of which you are more certain.

You can usually eliminate one of the choices in multiple choice questions easily. Try to approximate the right answer by "fuzzy logic" —by using whatever you can deduce from the information before you and then just make a calculated guess.

Don't overthink the problem.

If the question contains demographic data such as age, sex or race of the person, it might be an important bit of information when making your selection for the right answer.

In lengthy question statements, read the last two sentences first to see what information is being sought, and then read the question again from the beginning. Sort out the information that is relevant to the question posed at the end.

Sometimes, if you already know the answer to the question at the end, you may be able to save time by reading the rest of the question faster.

During the breaks in the exam, if there is a free period, try to avoid any deep dialogues with others and just take a walk, get a snack, or refreshment. Use any meditation techniques that you have learned; use any relaxation methods that have worked for you.

Avoid talking about the questions in the exam that you have just taken. It will only distract you and may demoralize you if you think your answer was wrong.

Do give an answer even for the questions that you are not sure of. There is no penalty on most exams for putting the wrong answer but an unanswered question is automatically counted wrong and goes against you.

Remember: You Are Not In A Race With Anyone

Remember that you are not in a race or contest with someone else. You are there to test your own knowledge.

If you don't get all the answers, don't be overcritical of yourself but try to learn from the errors that you made.

Don't worry about other people finishing first. Take your time and use the time that you have wisely.

Don't be tempted to always change the answers you have already given if you are not 100 percent sure.

Many of the answers that are changed end up being wrong and most of the original answers end up being right.

Don't over-read into a question but recognize the common tricks examiners like to use. I personally don't like questions which have the EXCEPT clause.

With practice, however, you can learn to recognize these tactics and will not be tricked or flustered by them. This is another reason that practice tests are so helpful.

If you have access to a question bank, subscribe to it and

practice as many questions as you can.

Always read the explanations, especially about the questions you got wrong.

Understand the reasons for a wrong answer so you can be right the next time.

The answer you got wrong will inevitably be asked in the test so it is important to read the correct answer to that question and master the required knowledge underlying the question.

A Restatement of Some Of The Strategies:

Prepare for the test and go over the materials by studying on a regular basis.

Do some physical exercises every day before the test.

Get a good night's rest before the day of the test.

Take a few deep breaths after every 10 questions during a test.

Get the easy questions done first and come back to the ones you have some doubts about.

Study sample questions, if available, first.

Read the question carefully, but don't over-read into it.

Read the last part of a long question first and then read the whole question.

If there are any clues about race or sex on tests of biological sciences, these are important clues in the question. You should pay attention to facts that pertain to that sex or race.

Read and understand as much of the question bank questions as you can.

If you have ADHD, take your medications as prescribed.

Some herbs such as Ashwaganda can be helpful for the stress of taking an exam.

Don't let any exam define who you are.

There are many exams we have to take twice. If you fail an exam, it will be ok. Don't exaggerate or catastrophize the consequences.

Imagine yourself doing well and walking out satisfied.

Do this visualization of succeeding once or twice a day whenever you get a chance.

Life is a series of exams. Play along as if it is a game. Play to the best of your ability but don't take it too seriously.

Don't worry about not doing well. Imagine yourself doing well and just do. Let everything else fall into its own place.

Words of Wisdom from The Jedi

In the legendary *Stars Wars Trilogy*, Yoda is the fictional character of a Jedi Master who teaches the hero of the movie Luke Skywalker on how to fight against evil. He admonishes the young Luke Skywalker thus:

"Do or Do not. There is no try."

It is great advice. You can apply this advice to taking exams.

"Do" the exam and that is all you need to do. There is no need to worry about the exam, just do the exam you have prepared for.

Get a good night's rest, arrive half an hour before the exam, maintain your silence and poise and avoid lengthy conversations.

You are prepared. Take a deep breath, and allow yourself to succeed almost effortlessly.

Just Do; There is No Try and Be Anxious Not

Chapter 15

Resources for Anxiety Treatment

The following associations can be resources for further information about anxiety disorders.

1. Anxiety and Depression Association of America (ADDA)

Website http://www.adaa.org/

2. National Institute of Mental Health (NIMH)

Website:

http://www.nimh.nih.gov/health/topics/anxiety-disorders/index.shtml

NIMH Mental Health Resource Center Tel 1-**888- 826-9438**

You can choose to be connected to a crisis line or be informed of resources for anxiety in your community.

3. National Alliance on Mental Illness (NAMI)

Website:

http://www.nami.org/template.cfm?section=anxiety_disorders

4. HelpGuide.org

Website

http://www.helpguide.org/index.htm

Finding Help In Your Community:

If you feel you are having problems with anxiety, the following persons may be worth talking to.

1. Your family doctor.

2. Local Mental Health Center: They often have sliding scale fees and try to be affordable. You may also qualify for no charge treatment.

3. If there is a local university, the department of psychology or psychiatry may have clinics that offer pro bono (free) or sliding scale fees for treatment.

4. In case of an emergency, you can call 911 and seek assistance at the local emergency rooms.

5. Your priest or pastor may offer counseling and may be aware of other resources in the community.

6. Local Transcendental Meditation Centers may be a resource for learning meditation. TM is a proven and highly effective intervention for managing stress. You can access their website at http://www.tm.org/. They can also be contacted at Phone 1-888-LEARN TM or (1-888-532-7686).

7. If you have insurance, the services of a trained and board certified psychiatrist are invaluable and should be sought whenever possible.

8. Local yoga classes maybe available and can also help with anxiety problems.

9. Local support groups for anxiety disorders may

meet where there are no fees and the members share their experiences and offer support to one another. Other members serve to offer validation and acceptance and some can be models of positive coping strategies.

What To Expect When You Are Referred To A Mental Health Professional:

The family doctor may refer you to a mental health professional such as a psychiatrist or a psychologist. If you are so referred, you should not be anxious about the meeting. Mental health professionals as a class tend to be compassionate and have a genuine interest in helping persons who suffer from anxiety or other emotional difficulties. A visit with one of these professionals can give you the ability to find relief from your symptoms and, in turn, gain confidence and control over your life.

It is useful to know the difference between a psychiatrist and a psychologist. Psychiatrists are medical doctors with specialized training in treating patients with mental illness. After finishing medical school, they devote four additional years in an accredited psychiatry residency training program.

Psychologists are doctors with a doctorate or PhD/PsyD in the area of psychology and are able to deliver every kind of mental health care aside from the prescription of medications, ECT or other medically based therapies.

The diagnosis of psychiatric disorders requires in all cases the ruling out of a medical cause of that condition. Since the psychiatrist is conversant with both the medical side of causation and the psychiatric pathology, he or she is often called upon to make the official psychiatric diagnosis.

A well-qualified psychiatrist will quickly recognize any medications and medical conditions that may be causing anxiety. He or she can suggest alternatives that will not have anxiety as a side effect. This step alone can sometimes solve the problem.

Most psychiatrists do provide supportive and other types of psychotherapy in addition to prescribing medications for psychiatric conditions. More often, the work of psychotherapy is shared with other clinicians. This combined approach has been shown by studies to be the most effective way of reducing anxiety or depression, and treating most other psychiatric symptoms.

When you go for your first meeting, you can expect to be asked about your medical history, your family psychiatric history, and any prior treatments.

The psychiatrist or psychologist will most likely also ask you about any significant physical or emotional trauma you may have experienced in the past. This is because emotionally traumatic events can cause lasting anxieties.

If you are placed on medication, ask about the risks and benefits of the medication. Keep your scheduled appointments and, if there are side effects, let your doctor know. If there are no side effects, you should continue and faithfully take the medication for the minimum recommended time period to realize the benefits. For most psychiatric medications, it means a period of at least 6 to 8 weeks. Once remission is attained, the medication is usually continued for at least a year in consultation with your doctor. Do not mix alcohol or other drugs with your medication. Check with your doctor when a new medication is added to see that there are no adverse interactions with your current medications.

Use one or more of the techniques you have learned for managing your anxiety and stress and stay faithful to your course of overcoming your anxiety symptoms.

Should you experience any adverse effects, or if suicidal ideations emerge at any time due to any reason, you should contact a mental health professional. If one is not available, go to the nearest emergency room.

As you have seen, there are a great many options for treating anxiety. It is possible to find an intervention that will work for you.

Epilogue

Anxiety Disorders and Depressive Disorders are real clinical conditions that cause significant amounts of distress and torment to the affected individuals and their families.

There is irrefutable evidence that pharmacological agents in the class of antianxiety and antidepressant agents help many such sufferers to climb out of the pits of their anxiety and despair. They are able to come back from the edge and resume useful roles in their families and in society.

It would be a disservice to a patient suffering from a biologically based anxiety disorder such as OCD to deny him or her medication that could correct the condition and bring about relief that psychotherapy alone could never provide.

Hence, we must remain pragmatic and eclectic in our approach and use whatever has been shown by objective evidence to work. Political passions or ideological demagoguery should play no role in the rational approach to treatment of serious mental disorders where human suffering or relief rests in the balance.

In this book you have been provided with some information about anxiety and its causes. We have also delved into the different treatment options that are available for anxiety related problems. This knowledge should help you to take the initiative to consult with your doctor or therapist about pursuing a course of treatment for decreasing your anxiety. It is simpler than you think and relief is possible.

Remember as well that, if someone is struggling with anxiety, it is not a sign of weakness. It often speaks of a sensitive and perceptive mind.

As you wage your battle with anxiety, you will be helped if you can let go of the need to win everyone's approval. In the best of circumstances, a significant number of people will disagree with you. If you were in fact able to convince 51 percent of the people to agree with you, you could be the elected head of state in a democratic country.

Learn to accept yourself at the deepest level. You don't need a model citizen certificate from anyone. As long as you are not harming anyone and as long as you are not violating the law, you have the right to be proud of who you are, proud of what you represent. We are all imperfect and yet perfect. Your self-acceptance is the first and the last step you will need to take towards ridding yourself of anxiety and its many woes.

You have a right to be free from anxiety and undue stress and to pursue happiness. Your suffering does not please God or anyone else. There is no honor in self-mortification; hence, a desire to get relief from anxiety is a sign of good mental health.

The beginnings of a new journey towards this anxiety-free life can start with a few simple steps, such as setting up an appointment to see your doctor about your concerns. If you take these first few steps, a brave new world awaits you with unlimited horizons of a fulfilled and peaceful life.

Prior to your visit with your doctor, write down some questions and be totally honest with him or her.

The information you share is protected under the strictest of confidentiality laws (unless what you reveal implies a danger to your own or someone else's safety).

You can consider and write down the options you want to explore. Perhaps you want to explore a trial of medication for the anxiety symptoms. Perhaps starting psychotherapy is the way you want to go first. Or perhaps you want your doctor's opinion on joining an exercise program, joining a yoga class, or learning to meditate for anxiety. You will be surprised how informed the modern trained physician is about such subjects.

Perhaps you want to read other books and get more information and try to analyze your own thoughts for any distortions and try to correct these on your own. Your doctor will be able to guide you in all of these options.

Just remember that help is available. When you start out, the progress will be small but it will be real and tangible. With a focus on clear thinking, you can start looking at everything from a perspective of whether the thought is distorted in any way. If you keep your thoughts clear and rational, the anxiety will give up and go away with time.

As you continue with the practice of "right thinking" that is free of distortions, your contentment and inner peace will gradually grow into a major healing force in your life.

So what we are saying is that you have the knowledge and understanding that you need. With this knowledge, you can try a number of different treatment plans to overcome anxiety. If one does not work, try another. Ask for help from professionals or others that you trust.

Sometimes, asking for help is the most intelligent thing you can do. If life throws you a curveball, hit that ball out of the ballpark. Make practical plans to overcome any anxiety that you have. Make plans to succeed despite any obstacles that may come your way. You can do it. You can achieve all that you dream of. By decreasing anxiety, you can increase the amount of happiness in your life.

Be Realistic: Make a Plan to Overcome Anxiety

TSG

Other Books By The Author

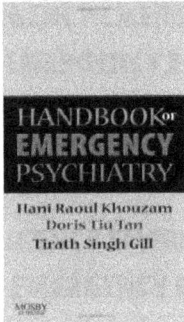

HANDBOOK OF EMERGENCY PSYCHIATRY

http://www.amazon.com/Handbook-Emergency-Psychiatry-Hani-Khouzam/dp/0323040888/ref=sr_1_1?ie=UTF8&qid=1399880616&sr=8-1&keywords=Tirath+s+gill+md

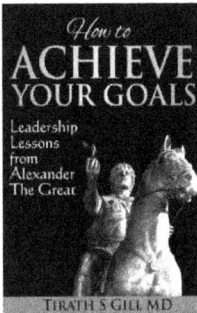

HOW TO ACHIEVE YOUR GOALS: LEADERSHIP LESSONS FROM ALEXANDER THE GREAT

http://www.amazon.com/How-Achieve-Your-Goals-Leadership/dp/0989664902/ref=sr_1_fkmr1_1?ie=UTF8&qid=1399880826&sr=8-1-fkmr1&keywords=Tirath+s+gill+md

Notes

Notes